Too Weird To

Be Fake!

Martin R. Shaw

"…we send those men up into space to unlock the doors of the universe, and we don't even know what's behind them."

-Fox Mulder; *The X-Files*

Table of Contents

PREFACE

In my opinion, when it comes to encounters with strange beings and entities, the weirder the better.

Sure, it's always fun to hear about a classic alien abduction case or Bigfoot sighting, but the stories that grab me are always the ones that are even weirder than that. Encountering a little grey guy from outer space or a big hairy dude in the forest is fine, but when someone runs into an eight-foot-tall, half biological–half robotic humanoid with four arms and twenty eyes that disappears in a puff of red smoke, that's when I really sit up and start to pay attention.

The reason for this is quite simple: Why would someone make it up? Why would anyone make up a tale that is so absolutely bizarre and beyond belief unless they were telling the truth? When someone's encounter with the unknown drifts into the realms of high strangeness (bizarre, surreal, absurd), this is when they start to become absolutely believable to me.

Here's the thing, though: when an encounter takes a detour into the world of high strangeness, it can sound absolutely ridiculous. Most investigators and interested parties will try to report, retell, and publish these encounters with a straight face. This isn't something I do. I lean into the weirdness. I make jokes. I reference pop culture. I try to make each story found in this book as engaging and entertaining as possible. Why? Because the supernatural, the paranormal, and the unexplained can be fun.

Sometimes I think it's fine to just throw conventional logic to the side, read a crazy story about extraterrestrial goblins attacking a farmhouse or a robotic clown chatting with some kids and say "Woah, that's weird!" There's a time and a place for official inquiries, the charting of weather patterns on the dates in question, and cross-examinations of witnesses. This book is neither the time nor the place. We're here to look at some stories that beg the question "Why make this up?" and have some fun along the way.

That's not to say that I don't take these encounters seriously. I believe that every one of these twenty tales has some truth to them. I believe that the people in these stories did indeed encounter something that they couldn't explain. In every story, the facts remain.

Along with these bizarre stories, I'll also be sharing popular theories that try to explain what actually happened. We'll look at theories from the point of view of the believers and the sceptics, along with some of my own radical ideas.

Will I be biassed in my retellings? Of course I will be. The normal, everyday world can be quite dull. As outlandish as many of these stories are, who does it hurt to ask "What if this is true?" While I might not actually believe every part of every story in this book, it's fun to imagine. To quote a famous FBI agent: "I want to believe." I prefer to live in a world of talking mongooses, telepathic aliens, and flying bigfoots (bigfeet?). If that means I have to suspend some disbelief, bend some truths, and ignore some facts in favour of a good story, that's what I'm going to do. You keep your boring reality; give me the gnomes from outer space!

All the stories in this book were researched from multiple sources. Many sources contradicted each other. Some sources even contradicted themselves. Some stories had gaps in their narrative. Some had big chunks that seemed to be entirely missing. Due to this, I've tried to piece each tale together in a way that either made the most sense to me, or was the most entertaining way to present it (I'm a big believer in "print the legend" and "never let the truth get in the way of a good story"). If you find any tale in particular piques your interest, I encourage you to go and do your own personal research. Form your own theories. Decide what version of events makes the most (or least) sense to you. But most of all, have fun with it!

Whether you're coming into this book ready to believe, whether you're a hardened sceptic who can't be swayed, or whether you're just looking to be entertained by some weird stories; you're in the right place.

Welcome to *Too Weird To Be Fake!*

INTRODUCTION

Throughout history, mankind has been subject to the type of strange encounters that cannot be explained by logic, reason, or science. Encounters of the supernatural, the paranormal, and the unexplainable.

These encounters, which once fascinated and mystified, have become so retold and similar that, despite their validity, they have become a part of normality. As time has marched on, these encounters have become tired, predictable, and even boring. These encounters began to follow a formula and a set plot, and their believability dwindled along with their credibility. Even if many of these run-of-the-mill encounters are true, we've heard them all before.

A hiker sees a hairy bipedal humanoid with a massive shoe size walking through the woods and we say "Oh, another one?" A family reports seeing the phantom of a dead loved one walk through a wall in their home and we say "Oh, just like in all the movies!" An unfortunate soul is taken aboard an interstellar craft against their will and experimented on by diminutive grey extraterrestrials and we say "Ugh, change the channel." This book is not about those encounters.

For every thousandth copied and pasted bigfoot sighting, poltergeist inhabitation, and alien abduction there is something truly unusual. Something out of the ordinary even in the world of the out of the ordinary. Some people aren't lucky enough to experience an everyday supernatural encounter; some get something far stranger. Something that, even in today's open-minded world, they struggle to recount for fear of ridicule, disbelief, and even harassment.

These people have bravely shared their stories. Stories that go so far into the realms of high strangeness that you have to ask "Why make this up?" Money? Fame? Many never tried to profit from their terrifying tales, and if money was the goal, there are hundreds of years' worth of material to steal from. Why come up with something so unheard of and unsellable, even to the most disconcerting of tabloids?

As for fame, many had their lives, both personal and professional, damaged or even ruined by sharing their unbelievable ordeals. Others stayed anonymous and remain anonymous to this day.

So if we take money and fame out of the equation, we're left with a frightening thought: what if these tales of mind-bending and terrifying supernatural surrealness are true?

This book is about those encounters.

The encounters that make you say:

"This is Too Weird To Be Fake!"

THE INDESCRIBABLE OCTOMAN & THE FROG PEOPLE

Nessie, Bigfoot, and the Chupacabra are cryptids we all know and love.

They've been around for centuries, and every so often they reappear in a new blurry photo, shaky video footage, or a harrowing eyewitness account before going back into hiding and leaving us wondering when they'll appear next.

For every famous cryptid that has a wealth of history, slews of eyewitnesses, decades of research, and armies of plush novelties made in their likeness, though, there are hundreds of lesser known weird beasts. These cryptids are no less strange than their more famous kin. In fact, many are far *more* strange, but they never make it to the big time.

The reason for this is that many of these cryptids only appear once or twice, and are only seen by a handful of people. They rarely leave any hard evidence, not even a footprint in the mud. No scientist, pseudo or otherwise, takes the time to do any real research. A couple of weeks after an encounter and short article in a local paper with an amusing headline, many of these creatures are totally forgotten about by everyone outside of the loose-knit but dedicated community of people with an interest in the unknown.

The main reason many of these cryptids never reach Bigfoot levels of fame is likely their appearance. Most are far less appealing than a prehistoric aquatic dinosaur, a furry humanoid, or a large fanged reptilian canine. These lesser-known cryptids are much more unbelievable, surreal, otherworldly, terrifying, disturbing, and…*indescribable.*

"Something came out of the river."

This is what the dispatcher for the Ohio's Clermont County and New Richmond Police Department heard when they answered the phone one night in January 1959. The dispatcher was understandably confused. They asked the man calling where he currently was and he told them that he was about four miles outside of New Richmond. They then asked him to explain what had happened. The man recounted how he had been walking along the banks of the Ohio River when he saw *something* emerge from the water and walk onto shore. The man presumably rushed to a nearby payphone, or somewhere with a phone, and called the police.

The dispatcher was still confused. They didn't know what they were dealing with. It didn't sound like any crime had been committed, but the man's concern seemed to be with what he saw coming out of the river. They asked the man to describe what exactly he had seen leaving the waters that had troubled him so. He panickedly told the dispatcher that what he had seen was not of this Earth. That it was simply "indescribable". Then he hung up without leaving a name or any personal details.

The dispatcher passed on the details of this anonymous call to the officers working that night. The officers didn't take the report too seriously. Probably a drunk or some kids pulling a prank, they thought. Besides, they didn't have enough information to really do anything. What were they meant to do, patrol miles of the Ohio River and its many tributaries looking for someone or something that was indescribable? But the officers hadn't heard what the dispatcher had heard on the phone. The officers hadn't heard the terror in the man's voice. The dispatcher knew that this was no drunken hallucination or highschool prank. The dispatcher didn't know how quickly they would be proved right.

Not long after the first report, another phone call came into the police station. This time it was from a truck driver who had pulled over at a gas station to report what he had seen. The truck driver was on his way towards Cincinnati when he saw something by the Little Miami River (a tributary of the Ohio River) from his cab. Much like the first call, the driver struggled to describe exactly what he had seen. All he could manage to say was that it looked like nothing he had ever seen before.

After this second call, the police started to take the sightings a bit more seriously. Officers went to a bridge near Kellogg Avenue, where the gas station was located, to investigate. As they arrived, all the streetlights cut out. The police found no trace of whatever had scared these men to the extent that they phoned to report it, and no more calls came in that night. They assumed it was case-closed.

They were wrong.

Somehow, the local press had found out about these two calls, and on the 29th of January the *Cincinnati Post & Times-Star* published an article titled "What Is It? 'Monster' Churns Up The Ohio". The article detailed the two calls and the strangely coincidental power outage that left the police in darkness just as they began to search.

Although the article was somewhat tongue in cheek, and featured the question "Anyone missing an 'indescribable monster' that swims?", the newspaper unexpectedly received a barrage of new reports. As it turns out, more people did see something strange that night, but most didn't think to phone the police. After reading the "What Is It?" article, these people realised that what they saw wasn't just in their imagination and they weren't alone. They decided to share their encounters with the *Cincinnati Post*.

The next day, January 30, the newspaper ran a followup article. Whoever came up with headlines at the paper struck gold for the second time in two days with the great title; "Driver Swears It Happened: River Monster Takes a Stroll On Bridge". In this article, an anonymous man explains how, on the very same night as the two calls to the police and the power outage, he was driving over a bridge that crossed the Licking River (yet another tributary of the Ohio River).

As he drove across, suddenly something leapt from the water and landed on the bridge a few metres ahead of his car. Although he saw the creature only briefly, he claims he got a good look at it as he drove past. He described it as being taller than his vehicle, three or four times the size of a normal man, and much bulkier. He went on to claim that it definitely wasn't a cat or a dog, and bragged that he has a particular eye for dimensions so would not be mistaken in this fact.

Another report came in from a young woman who claimed to have seen the creature in a creek near a pumping station close to the Ohio River. She described the creature as looking like an octopus, marking the first time this creature would get a cephalopod-like description and earn it the name of Octoman.

There was one further sighting that would give us the clearest picture of the Octoman and finally give a description to the indescribable. Five miles away in Covington, a woman claimed to have seen the Octoman hunched over by the Ohio River, and the description she gave of the creature could have come straight out of H.P. Lovecraft's Cthulhu Mythos.

She described the creature as being humanoid, having green-grey skin, a lopsided chest, and being totally bald. She said it had rolls of fat running over its smooth head and tentacles in place of arms, cementing the image of an octopus humanoid in the public's imagination. The fact that now two seemingly unrelated witnesses had given this creature an octopus-like description seemed far too coincidental to have been made up.

After this final and most detailed encounter and description of the Octoman, though, he seemed to vanish just as quickly as he arrived, returning to his underwater hiding place or to whatever strange reality he came from.

What was the Indescribable Octoman? Was it an animal species undiscovered by science? If it was, then why were there no reported sightings before or since? Even if it was an extremely rare creature, the only one of its kind, it seems unlikely that there would never be any more sightings.

Could the Octoman have been an extraterrestrial? Its bizarre appearance certainly seems out of this world. Although no UFO sightings were reported in the area before, during or after the Octoman encounters, the theory that it was an alien is a popular one. Many believe that Octoman was the survivor of a crashed UFO, left wandering the local area until it was either rescued by more of its species, scooped up by a government agency and carted off to Area 51 for a classic alien autopsy, or simply died from injuries sustained in the crash and washed downriver never to be seen again.

Could the Octoman be something entirely mundane and explainable? Many sceptics at the time suggested that witnesses had simply seen an oddly shaped piece of driftwood floating down the Ohio River that they mistook for a creature in the poor lighting. While this case of mistaken identity sounds believable enough, driftwood tends to not have tentacles and it rarely leaps onto bridges.

It also seems unlikely that two entirely different people would mistake driftwood for a creature beyond their description and become so troubled by the sight that they phoned the police.

The police were also working on a mistaken identity theory, but one that was more human and less driftwood. Some of the officers believed that what people were seeing was a victim of a car accident. They believed it may have just been a regular human, hurt and disoriented, wandering around a stretch of the Ohio River. No crashed car was reported or found, no injured person was discovered or admitted to hospital, and no one was reported missing. Besides this, a car accident certainly wouldn't make a regular person increase in mass and grow a collection of tendrils.

A theory that connects Octoman to many other of our favourite cryptids is that it came from another dimension. Many believe that Nessie, Bigfoot, and the Chupacabra travel to our world from their home dimension, but they have some control on how, when, and where they get here. The theory goes that other lesser seen and reported cryptids simply fall into our reality against their will and then return at random.

Could the Octoman have been minding his own business in his own world when suddenly a terrifying vortex ripped a hole in the fabric of space and time, sucked him through, and dropped him off in a river outside of New Richmond, Ohio? Did Octoman wander around, confused as to where he was and what had happened to him, before being sucked right back through? Perhaps he tried to explain what had happened to other members of his cephalopod species, only to be met with disdain and ridicule.

Believers in this interdimensional theory point to the power cut as possible evidence towards it. They say that when some sort of tear between dimensions opened to bring Octoman back home, it created a type of electromagnetic interference that caused the streetlights on Kellogg Avenue to cut out — the streetlights very close to where Octoman was spotted by the truck driver the night of the sightings.

The idea that cryptids, UFOs, ghosts, and all manner of supernatural and paranormal beings and creatures come from another realm and occasionally slip into ours is a popular theory. Many paranormal authors suggest that the barrier between dimensions and realities is like a veil, and there are places where the veil is thinner and even has tears. These places where the veil gets thin become paranormal hotspots, places where UFOs are seen in the sky, weird creatures are spotted, and poltergeist activity takes place. Could the veil be thin or torn somewhere in the Ohio River? It may seem unlikely if Octoman was the only weird creature reported here…but he isn't.

In 1955, four years before Octoman turned up, a woman was taking a dip in the river with a friend. Suddenly, the woman's leg was grabbed by a large clawed hand that attempted to drag her beneath the surface. She escaped the grasp multiple times, only to be pulled under once again. She managed to struggle free a final time, and reached the river bank with the help of her friend who was on an inner tube, but on her leg was left a mark of the hideous hand that had tried to drown her. The hand/claw print was curiously and unexplainably green. The woman never got a look at what manner of beast could possess such a hand, but it just might have been a frog person.

Also in 1955, along one of the Ohio Rivers tributaries, a businessman named Robert Hunnicutt reported seeing three strange creatures. He described them as being between three and four feet tall, having pale green leathery flesh, thin arms, webbed hands and feet, and frog-like heads. The man watched these creatures for around three minutes, until one of them held something that looked like a wand above its head which started to erupt blue sparks from one end. The man left sharpish as the magical sparkler show began.

The frog people reappeared in 1973 when a Loveland police officer almost ran one down in his squad car. It was 1.00 AM and the officer was out on patrol near the Little Miami River when something ran out into the road. He slammed on the breaks and the vehicle came screeching to a halt. Like a frog in the headlights, the animal froze. Standing between three and four feet tall was what looked like a cross between man and amphibian. Before the officer could get out and question the creature, it leapt off the road and into the river. Luckily it wasn't armed with its magic wand.

The frog cryptids have been spotted many times over the years, and even as recently as 2016. Two teens were out playing the newly released augmented reality game *Pokémon Go* on their mobile phones when they stumbled upon a monster that seemed to belong in their game, and not in the real world. The teens saw what they described as a giant frog standing on its hind legs, like a human. Had they just mistaken one of the amphibian-based creatures from their game, like Seismitoad or Poliwrath, for a creature in real life? Was the AR in this new and cutting edge mobile game so good that the teens mistook fantasy for reality? They swear this isn't the case.

These creatures have become known as the Loveland Frogmen and have become quite famous cryptids in their own right. The croaking cryptids have even spawned (pun intended) their own local festival, just like their monstrous peers Mothman and Braxxie.

With such an array of weirdness in and around the Ohio River in the 1950s alone, if there is a tear between this world and a dimension full of strange octopus and frog humanoids, it may be found somewhere here, in the deep, dark depths of this long and winding river.

SAM: THE SANDOWN CLOWN

C lowns, though meant to bring entertainment and joy, are a source of terror to many.

Coulrophobia, the fear of clowns, is one of the most common phobias in the world today, but it's hard to pinpoint exactly why. Does the facepaint, giant nose, and wild hair conjure feelings of something otherworldly? Something humanoid but not quite human? Is it the erratic nature of the clown that makes it untrustworthy? While it may be the case that the appearance and mannerisms of the clown triggers fear in people alone, the main culprit behind this phobia in the modern age is likely pop culture.

Pennywise, the evil clown from Stephen King's novel *IT*, and its subsequent TV and film adaptations, inspired fear across multiple generations. Anyone who was a child in the 1990s and visited a video shop can likely tell you how they were mentally scarred when they saw the VHS cover art for *IT*, featuring a greasepaint-slathered Tim Curry ripping his way out of the box design with demonic hands. This fear was built upon by a parade of cinematic evil clowns that followed; from the silent slasher Art from the *Terrifier* films to the chicken-frying Captain Spaulding from *House of 1000 Corpses*.

In real life, clowns have been no less of a threat to our senses. In 2016, there was an epidemic of "evil clown" sightings. In the UK, USA, and Canada, people began seeing creepy clowns in areas such as car parks, wooded areas, and even next to schools. Sometimes they just stood there, sometimes they were very animated. Sometimes they had balloons, sometimes they had knives. Some witnesses managed to get photos and videos of these clowns on their phones, and the phenomenon quickly exploded on social media. Soon people from all over the world were reporting seeing clowns everywhere.

It wasn't long before a sort of panic took hold. Several universities in America started "clown hunts". Mobs were formed with the intention of hunting down a clown after a supposed sighting took place. On Halloween that year, some people allegedly went trick or treating armed for self defence against these horrible harlequins.

In an attempt to stem the tide of clowns, and to stop anyone innocent from being hurt, fancy dress shops started to stop the sale of clown costumes. Bans on clown outfits and masks were put in place. The World Clown Association issued a statement claiming that this creepy clown epidemic had hurt the honest and hard working everyday clowns' businesses and income. Even the McDonald's mascot, Ronald, had to take a back seat until this new prejudice died down.

Soon after 2016, the sightings started to dwindle, and people started to calm down and look at the whole thing rationally. Outside of a few photos and video clips, there was no evidence to suggest that the clown encounters were nearly as vast and widespread as previously claimed.

It's believed that the initial sightings started either as viral marketing for an upcoming horror movie, or just a simple internet prank. Soon a few copycats were inspired and their own antics made it onto the internet, probably captured on the phones of friends in on the joke and not terrified bystanders as they claimed. This caused the clown sightings to grow. More people got involved, reporting unsubstantiated sightings and throwing fuel onto the fire, and before we knew it we had a "clown epidemic" that didn't really exist, and a beloved fast food mascot had to take a brief but involuntary redundancy. Although the media often referred to this as a "killer clown epidemic" or something similar, there were no verified reports that any clown had attacked anyone, let alone killed them.

The fear of a *real* killer clown came much earlier than 2016. In late 1978, serial killer John Wayne Gacy was apprehended and discovered to have killed at least thirty-three young men and boys. As if this wasn't horrific enough, when it was combined with one of his hobbies it truly inspired nightmares. In his spare time he liked to perform as his alter ego, Pogo the Clown. He performed at children's hospitals, charity events, parties, and even in parades. While he was entertaining friends, family, and his community with his clowning he was also engaging in some of the most horrific murders ever reported. Ever since this hobby was discovered by the media, he has been known by the infamous nickname of "The Killer Clown".

Whether fictional, rumoured, or entirely real — clowns have scared us. But not all clowns have the intention of terrifying their observers. Sometimes their intentions are far more strange and unknowable. In the summer of 1973, on the Isle of Wight, two children had their own encounter with a clown. An encounter so bizarre and surreal that it cannot help but be believed.

A boy and a girl, both around seven years old, were on holiday in the seaside town of Sandown near Lake Common with their families. Though the lake was Common, their day would not be. The pair were off by themselves, playing and exploring the area, at around 4.00 PM on a Tuesday. Suddenly, they heard an odd noise. They described it as a wailing sound, similar to an ambulance siren.

This unexpected sound made them curious, and they decided to follow it and try to find its source. They followed the wailing across a golf course and towards a swampy meadow close to the rarely-used Sandown Airport. As they reached this area, the sound suddenly stopped. The kids, now more curious than ever to find the source, reasoned that it must have been coming from within this marshland and decided to head on.

They ventured deep into this marshy and boggy area and eventually came across an old wooden footbridge that crossed a brook. As they stepped onto this bridge, the unbelievable happened. The kids saw a hand wearing a blue glove reach up from underneath the bridge. A hand that had only three fingers. The owner of the hand then appeared from under, and it was no less strange. In fact, to the children, it looked a little bit like a clown.

It was humanoid in appearance. It was seven feet tall. It had no neck and its head simply sat on his shoulders. It wore a yellow pointy hat with a round black knob or dial on it. The hat had antennae protruding from either side. It wore a green tunic with a red collar. What looked like pieces of wood stuck out from its sleeves and the bottom of its white trousers. As if this wasn't jester-like enough, it was its face that really earned this creature the name of "The Sandown Clown". It had blue triangle markings for eyes, a brown square for a nose, and yellow lips. Its face was extremely white with round black markings on its cheeks, and it had a fringe of red/brown hair that poked out of its yellow hat.

The children were surprised to see such a funny looking figure, but they felt no fear of it. The humanoid was carrying some sort of book and seemed to be struggling to keep a hold of it. Understandable, due to it only having three fingers. Sure enough, the book slipped from its hands and it landed in the brook below the bridge. The Sandown Clown quickly jumped back down to retrieve its lost property. It fished around, found the book, and the kids watched as it hopped off to a small windowless metal hut nearby and entered.

While this encounter would have been enough to send any adult, suffering from coulrophobia or not, running off the entire Isle of Wight, the kids — being kids — didn't realise how weird this all was. They just thought "Don't see that everyday!"

With the clown gone, the children were confused and unsure of what to do, but not feeling afraid, they just slowly wandered off. When they had gotten about fifty yards away from the bridge, the clown-like humanoid appeared again. This time it was carrying something that looked like a black microphone with a white cable. As soon as the Sandown Clown reappeared, the wailing sound began again.

Now the strangeness of what was happening had hit the kids, and they started to run away. When they had covered a small distance, the wailing stopped and they heard a voice. A voice that sounded like it was right next to them, although it could not possibly have been. The voice asked "Hello, are you still there?" The kids stopped running. They knew the voice belonged to the figure they were running from, probably being amplified by its microphone. They both decided that the voice sounded friendly enough, and that it would be rude to not go back for a chat. Good old British manners.

The kids turned around and walked back towards the figure, still understandably slightly nervous about the whole situation. When they were back in sight of the clown, it produced a notebook (possibly the same book it dropped in the water earlier) and wrote in it. It held up what it had written and…it didn't make any sense.

They were English words, but they were nonsense. The words were out of order and didn't form a coherent sentence. That was when the figure began pointing at the individual words with one of its three fingers, and the girl realised that it wanted her to read them in the order it pointed at them. The girl read aloud as it pointed: "Hello and I am all colours, Sam." The kids exchanged confused looks and walked closer to Sam. As they got closer, Sam began to communicate verbally, which was easier than pointing at words in a book, but no less strange. When Sam spoke, his yellow lips did not move. His voice sounded muffled and was hard to understand.

The kids began to ask Sam questions. They noticed that his clothes had some rips in them, so they asked why. Sam told them that they were the only clothes he owned. A bit rude to bring it up in the first place, in my opinion.

With questions of fashion out of the way, the kids got down to the hard hitting topics. Sam's unusual appearance was not lost on them, and they wanted to know what he was. They asked "Are you a man?" Sam replied matter of factly; "No." They then asked, I'm sure with some nervousness: "Are you a ghost?" Sam answered vaguely, "Not really, but I am in an odd sort of way." The kids were confused and asked "What are you then?" Sam gave a vague response; "You know." and in a move reminiscent of David Lynch refused to elaborate further. Sam also told the kids that there were more beings like him but didn't give any information on where to find them. He alluded to being afraid humans would attack him and, being a pacifist, he would not fight back if they did.

Now that everyone was good friends, Sam invited the kids to join him in his metal hut that they had seen earlier. They wandered back towards the bridge and followed Sam inside his home by crawling through a small flap. The hut had two levels; the ground floor had wooden furniture, an electric heater, and wallpaper that was decorated in a dial pattern. The first floor had less headroom and a metal floor. Sam proudly told the kids he built the hut himself.

The kids had some more questions for Sam. They wanted to know what he ate and drank. He told them that the water from the nearby brook was safe to drink after being cleaned. For food, he ate berries that he foraged. He then gave the kids a little demonstration of the unexpected way he ate these berries. First he put a berry in his ear. Then he moved his head in such a way that the berry disappeared from his ear and reappeared in his triangular eye. He then moved his head again and the berry appeared in his yellow lips. Whether he ate like this all the time or if he was just showing off for his new friends is unknown.

After half an hour, the kids decided that it was time to head back to their families, and Sam graciously let them leave his hut. They headed back through the marshy area and onto the golf course. As they passed an adult, they told him that they had just seen a ghost. The man did not believe them. Perhaps it was this man's dismissal of the tale that kept the kids from telling anyone else about Sam for a few weeks.

Three weeks after her encounter with the Sandown Clown, the young girl did tell her father the whole weird story. Her father was initially sceptical of his daughter's tale of meeting this strange clown figure just across a golf course from where they were holidaying, but her insistence that the story was real and her clear memory of all the details eventually started to win him over. He was even able to speak to the boy and found that his story matched up.

After many retellings and questioning, in which the young girl's story did not change, her father became convinced that she and the boy did encounter something out of the ordinary that day. He initially thought that it was maybe just a person in a costume who was out to scare kids. He quickly dismissed this theory, though, as creating an elaborate costume and building a metallic hut structure seemed like far too much effort for someone to go to just for a prank.

He decided to contact the British UFO Research Association (or BUFORA for short).

While it's easy to guess why he contacted BUFORA — Sam did seem like some sort of alien — the reason may be a bit more personal. The father had two strange experiences himself in the years prior to his daughter meeting the Sandown Clown. Experiences that may have made him well aware of the organisation.

Three years earlier, in October of 1970, he had seen a UFO while driving which followed him for some distance. Two years after that, while sitting on some cliffs at a bay, the father had seen a large pair of glowing yellow eyes looking up at him from the ocean. Could experiences with the supernatural run in the family?

With these memories of alien crafts and salt water monsters fresh in his mind, it's clear why he took his daughters' claims so seriously when others may have simply dismissed them as fantasy. It also explains why he might have had BUFORA on speed dial.

BUFORA listened to the girl's story and her father's insistence that his daughter was not lying. They investigated the story of Sam but found little evidence. They searched the area but found no clown and no hut. No one in the area they questioned had ever seen, or heard of anyone else seeing, a bizarre robotic alien clown in the area. Despite the lack of physical evidence or witnesses, BUFORA was convinced by the kid's story.

In the January/February issue of the *BUFORA Journal* in 1978, the story of Sam; The Sandown Clown, was finally shared with the world. A now iconic black and white drawing of Sam based on the kids' description made the cover, along with the eye-catching headline "GHOST or spaceman?" Sam had reached the imagination of the general public and became one more clown to cause fear and terror.

Sam has certainly stayed in the minds of many since he had his big cover story in 1978, but as well as inspiring fear (unjustly I'd say; he seemed pretty nice) he has also inspired a slew of theories that have tried to explain what exactly the two kids saw in the marshy meadow that day.

Sceptics have said that Sam was simply a man in a costume. Much like the girl's father, Sam believers have countered this with the question "why would someone do that?" If it was simply a normal human in a strange costume trying to freak out some kids, why go to this level of effort? Not to mention that Sam never *tried* to scare the children. The only time the kids felt scared was when he appeared the second time with his microphone device, but they did not say he tried to scare them. In fact, when he spoke to them with his microphone they were so convinced he was nothing to fear that they went back to have a chinwag with him.

Others have taken a darker view of Sam, believing he was a man in a suit, but he wasn't trying to scare children...he was trying to abduct them. While a seven-foot-tall clown inviting two young kids into his makeshift hut in the woods certainly raises a number of redflags, Sam never acted threateningly. The kids entered Sam's home on their own free will, and were allowed to leave when they wanted to without incident. Sam never showed any intention or desire to scare or harm the kids in any way, shape, or form. And if Sam was simply a man in an elaborate costume, it doesn't explain the wailing sound that drew the kids to him in the first place.

People who do not believe in a single piece of the Sandown Clown story claim the two kids were just making the whole thing up. They say the kids were likely bored and just wanted attention. If this were the case, why would the girl wait three whole weeks before telling her father? And after she began getting attention, and even getting interviewed by BUFORA, why would she, and the young boy, remain anonymous *to this day?* After the story began getting attention in 1978, there must have been plenty of opportunities to do more interviews with UFO journals and even newspapers and TV shows (which likely would have been paid) but they did nothing. Attention may have been something the kids got after meeting Sam, but it doesn't seem like something they wanted.

If Sam wasn't just a strange man in a costume, or a total fabrication, what else could he have been? Could Sam have been some sort of alien being? With his weird appearance and mannerisms, it seems an obvious conclusion to jump to. He doesn't resemble the traditional "Little Green Man" we usually think of when we picture an extraterrestrial, but alien descriptions have run the gamut of bizarre appearances. From the very human-looking Nordic descriptions of ETs, to the praying mantis resembling Insectoids, aliens have been reported to look like just about anything you can imagine. Sometimes they have mandibles, claws, antennae, tentacles, and more features typically not found on your average four-foot-high grey humanoid with big black eyes from beyond the stars.

Sometimes aliens are even reported to be partially robotic, which some think could explain the Sandown Clown. Some believe that Sam could have been an alien that was also a cyborg. They believe that the strange markings on his "clown suit", hat, and face were in fact dials and controls for his more mechanical parts, similar to Darth Vader's chest plate in the *Star Wars* movies. Could Sam have been a bionic Bozo?

Another theory suggests that Sam was indeed an alien, but was in a special suit. Perhaps a suit that allowed the alien to survive on Earth, similar to one of our own astronauts in outer space. They also believe that the reason behind his odd face and motionless lips is because the face the kids were seeing was actually a helmet or mask. If this is the case then who knows what manner of alien entity was inside this special suit that, unbeknownst to him, made him look a little bit like a circus clown.

Some have suggested that Sam was a ghost. It seems to be the conclusion that the kids came to, and Sam did say he was one (but also that he wasn't; he wasn't very clear on that). Many disagree with this theory, arguing that Sam simply doesn't follow the same format as other tales of ghosts and spectres. From appearing in broad daylight, to looking like a robotic clown, to having a metal hut for a home, some say Sam simply doesn't fit into the world of ghosts. As for Sam claiming that he is a ghost in "an odd sort of way", people believe that he was simply trying to make the kids understand something that was far beyond their capability by putting himself into terms they could understand.

Could Sam have been a creature not from another world, but from another dimension? Many authors on the paranormal and supernatural believe that there are places where there are tears in our reality that lead to another dimension where UFOs, ghosts, and cryptids dwell and occasionally slip though. Could the young boy and girl have briefly stepped through into another dimension? Or did Sam slip through into ours? Was the wailing sound the noise of an interdimensional portal tearing open? Was the wail a sound beamed directly into the brains of the children to bring them to Sam so he could study them and bring the data back to his dimension?

When it comes to explaining what Sam was, the young girl's father may have been right from the very beginning. The father told BUFORA that he believed his daughter and the boy had been "taken into a bubble of alien reality".

The Oz Factor is a phrase coined by ufologist Jenny Randals to describe the odd feeling many people who had experienced the unknown were reporting. Ufologists had noticed that in many reports of people encountering UFOs, extraterrestrials, and other strange beings, the experiencer described feeling displaced and isolated. They felt as if they were still in their own world but somehow different, like Dorothy in *The Wizard of Oz*. There were small but subtle and surreal differences: time seemed to move differently. There was a feeling of weightlessness. No sounds could be heard. No one else could be seen. Cats chased dogs. Some believe this effect is something caused (on purpose or as an unintentional side effect) by otherworldly beings who enter our reality. Could Sam have sucked the kids into their own alien land of Oz?

And what about the kids? Do they still remember their meeting with Sam all these years later? Did he have any lasting impact on their lives? Will they ever come forward and share their story again? As adults, maybe they understand what happened more clearly. Maybe they remember more details about what happened that day. Maybe they have a vital piece of information that could help us truly understand what Sam was.

When the kids asked Sam quite directly what he was and he replied with the very Lynchian "You know", what if he wasn't just being intentionally and annoyingly vague? What if Sam knew that the kids subconsciously understood exactly what he was? Maybe the two kids didn't even fully understand at the time, and certainly lacked the frames of reference and language skills necessary to convey to someone else exactly what this strange clown man was. Maybe it took years of mental processing for these kids to unlock the secret of the clown, but perhaps one day all the pieces fell into place and the kids finally understood.

Is it possible that the kids, now both well into middle age, are out there somewhere right now existing as the only two people on planet Earth who know the secret of Sam; The Sandown Clown?

Despite the only witnesses being two seven-year-old children, their story of meeting a semi-robotic alien clown–looking humanoid on the Isle of Wight in 1973 has endured ever since and still captures the imagination of those who hear it. Surely this has something to do with the public's built in fear of clowns, but it goes deeper than that. The young girl's father thought so, and so did BUFORA when they investigated it. They thought "This is *Too Weird To Be Fake!*"

ATTACK OF THE HOPKINSVILLE GOBLINS

I t's hard to imagine a goblin as anything other than a staple of classic fantasy media.

From J.R.R. Tolkien's masterpiece *The Lord of the Rings*, to every teenage social misfits bible, Dungeons & Dragons, these short, green, subterranean creatures feature in all. Although descriptions and motivations change slightly between interpretations, one feature remains: goblins are evil.

In every iteration, goblins are the antagonist. Whether they are chasing the Fellowship of the Ring through the Dwarven Mines of Moria or slaying a first level paladin through dice rolls, goblins are never on the side of good. When goblins make the jump from fantasy to reality, little changes. They still seem intent on terrorising whoever they run into.

In 1955, a farmhouse in Kentucky was right in the path of a brigade of real life rampaging goblins.

It was the night of August 21 in a small farmhouse near Hopkinsville owned by the Sutton family. The Suttons were hosting a little get together that evening. They had some extended family over with their kids, and their friend Billy Ray Taylor and his wife. In total there were eleven people in the house that night. The Sutton family and friends had no way of knowing that at that very moment something from another planet was making its way to Earth, and it had its sights set firmly on the humble little farmhouse.

At around 7.00 PM, most of the adults were in the kitchen, chatting and playing cards, while the children were in another room. It was a nice relaxed evening, full of laughter and reminiscing, but all that was soon to change. Billy Ray excused himself from the kitchen table, telling everyone he was off to get a drink of water from the well in the backyard. The card game had gotten intense and he needed quick rehydration in order to continue, but that's *Snap* for you. The Sutton farmhouse had no running water or indoor plumbing (or even a telephone, radio, or TV). What the home lacked in luxuries though, it was about to make up for in terror.

He made the short walk across the yard to the well. Billy Ray picked up a cup and began pumping some water into it. As he pumped, he gazed into the early evening sky. A meteor shower was reported to occur that night and Billy Ray hoped he could catch a glimpse of it. What he saw was no meteor.

As he finished pumping his drink and went to take a sip, he saw a flying saucer in the darkening sky. He described it as looking like a metallic silver in colour and had rainbow coloured flames shooting out of what he assumed was the craft's exhaust. The UFO flew right over the farmhouse then stopped in midair, hanging silently in the sky. He dropped his cup of water in shock, and as it fell to the ground so too did the flying saucer begin its descent to Earth. It landed out of sight in a field about 100 yards behind the Sutton farmhouse. Billy Ray could hear a soft hissing noise as the craft landed. Understandably, he ran back to the house.

Billy Ray was out of the house only briefly before he quickly re-entered. When he got back in, he slammed the door behind him and locked it shut. Everyone in the kitchen took notice as Billy Ray seemed terrified. He was out of breath and sweating, as if he'd sprinted back inside as quickly as he could.

"Are you alright?" they asked him, and he told them what had gotten him so worked up. Whatever answer they were expecting, it wasn't this. Billy Ray explained that as he was pumping some water from the well he saw a craft from another planet and it landed nearby.

He told the family the whole story of the silver saucer with rainbow exhaust, and no one believed him. Head of the household Elmer Sutton thought that Billy Ray had overreacted to seeing a falling star or was trying to get out of a game he was losing (the next time you're losing at a game, try saying there's a UFO outside). Billy Ray continued telling and retelling his story, insisting that he was serious, but he was getting through to no one. Eventually he just dropped the whole thing and took a seat, defeated. No one was even interested enough to take the short walk to investigate the possible alien landing site.

Around one hour later, the family were suddenly distracted from their conversations and card games by noises from outside. In the yard, the family dog was going wild, barking constantly. This was very uncharacteristic for the dog, and the family assumed it was in danger. Elmer quickly crossed to the window and looked out. Night had now fallen and it was dark outside, but it didn't take much strain for Elmer to see what was out there annoying his dog. What he saw was a silver and glowing object that seemed to be coming straight towards the house.

Elmer weighed his options. He thought through the variables. He considered his possible actions and the consequences they may bring. "What is this thing approaching my home? Is it a danger to my friends and family?" he thought. A thousand possibilities raced through his head. As he saw it, there was but one option: Elmer grabbed his gun, and he told Billy Ray to do the same. Elmer headed outside and Billy Ray followed him, both now heavily armed.

As soon as they got outside, the dog ran past them and into the house. It had given up its aggression towards the glowing object, and now hid in fear. As the glowing thing got closer, Elmer and Billy Ray realised that the glow was emanating from some sort of creature. It was almost as if it was radiating the silver colour, as if it glowed in the dark.

The glowing creature they described approaching the farmhouse was around three and a half feet high. It had a large, oversized head that was almost totally round. It had big yellow eyes that also seemed to glow. It had pointy ears. Its limbs were long and thin, and its hands were clawed. It had a thin mouth that extended to almost the entire width of its spherical head. Its skin (or whatever it was wearing over its skin) glowed with a silver hue. To the two men, it looked like a goblin. The creature was holding its arms in the air as it approached the house. While some may have seen this pose as a gesture of friendship, Elmer did not. He and Billy Ray opened fire on the small glowing humanoid.

The creature was hit by bullets from a 12-gauge shotgun and .22 rifle in a scene not unlike the origin of *RoboCop*. This barrage of lead would have been enough to take down any human or animal, but the small creature simply did a fancy backflip and ran off into the nearby woods. The men were adamant that they had hit their target, and hadn't just rolled critical fails while attacking this fantasy creature, it just seemed that the bullets had not hurt it in the slightest. The men said that it sounded like their bullets were hitting a metal surface, suggesting it was wearing some sort of body armour.

Elmer and Billy Ray exchanged shocked looks and headed back inside. "What's going on out there!?" family members cried. They tried to explain what had happened and calm everyone down, but were cut short. As they were talking, another creature that looked very similar to the first had appeared at a window. The women screamed. The children cried. The men opened fire. The window exploded from the gunfire, and glass shards rained. The creature at the window, once again seemingly unhurt, simply did a little flip and ran off.

Unsure of what to do next, Elmer and Billy Ray decided to head back outside. They intended to look for the corpses of the creatures they had shot. Although they seemed unharmed initially, they thought that they had maybe succumbed to their bullet wounds and died somewhere nearby. Wishful thinking.

Billy Ray stepped out onto the back porch, followed by Elmer, while the family watched in suspense from the doorway. Billy Ray stepped slowly and quietly, trying his best not to attract any attention from creatures he knew were still out in the darkness. He kept his shotgun up, ready to fire at anything that moved or glowed. He reached the end of the porch and was about to step out onto the grass when Elmer and the family saw something terrifying.

From the tin roof above the porch, a clawed hand reached down. Billy Ray hadn't noticed it, and by the time he heard the shouts of warning, it was too late. The clawed hand grabbed Billy Ray by the hair. Luckily, Elmer was able to run forwards, grab Billy Ray, free him of the goblin's grasp, and drag him back towards the door. Elmer, fueled by a lust for vengeance, ran back out of the house and into the yard. He spun around and shot at the creature on the roof, bullets ripping through the tin and striking the thing in the chest. The creature fell from the roof, but slowly. It seemed to float down to the ground in slow motion, in an almost sarcastic response to the man's aggression. Once again, this creature seemed unhurt by the bullet that had just struck its body. Elmer darted back into the house, but before the door was slammed shut he noticed *another* one of these creatures hanging out in a tree.

They locked the house down. The children were put to bed, though sleeping was hard due to the fear of glow-in-the-dark aliens and the constant sound of gunfire and screaming. In one last effort to deter the extraterrestrial invaders, Elmer and Billy Ray tried to shoot the creature that was spotted in the tree. They hit it either with expert accuracy or just firing so much that they couldn't feasibly miss. When struck with lead, this one also floated to the ground as if it had some sort of control over gravity. As it slowly fell, *another* creature casually ran across the lawn, as if daring the men to shoot it. Billy Ray and Elmer had finally realised that shooting these creatures was just a waste of ammo. They retreated into the farmhouse and hunkered down with their families, ready for a night of goblins.

Over the next three hours, the Sutton family and co. heard noises on the roof. It was the scraping sound of the goblinoids' claws as they crawled over the house, trying to find a way in. The creatures were seen sneaking up to the windows and peering through, only to flee when a scream went out or a gun was pointed. Though they seemed impervious to bullets, being shot at did seem to deter the goblins for at least for a short while. The families claim that during this time locked inside the house, the creatures tried to gain entry no less than six times.

When it reached 11.00 PM, the family had had enough. They couldn't take anymore harassment from these strange creatures, and besides they were running low on ammunition. They decided that their pointy-eared enemies could have the farmhouse. Elmer and Billy Ray got each of the families to the front door and told them that on the count of three they were going to run to the two cars in the driveway. They counted down, and the families fled the farmhouse and piled into the vehicles. Luckily the creatures hadn't thought to destroy the car engines, and the cars hadn't been hit by any stray bullets. The family sped away from the house and straight to the nearest police station in Hopkinsville.

The family arrived at the station and frantically told their story to police chief Russell Greenwell. Greenwell normally might not have taken this story of a landed UFO and a small army of glowing goblin invaders seriously, but he could tell that *something* had happened to these people that night. He described them as being terrified on arrival, and noted that they weren't the type of people who would normally come to the police for help.

Greenwell took some officers and drove over the Sutton farmhouse to investigate. Instantly, the police knew that something had happened here. Bullet shells and casing were found littering the grounds around the house, proof that Billy Ray and Elmer had been shooting at something. The house itself showed more evidence of the firefight. More casings were found inside, windows were blown out, and bullet holes were scattered around the walls and ceiling. The police could not find any evidence of the three-foot-tall terrors that the family described however.

Greenwell and his officers returned to the station and told the group that there was no sign of any intruders, terrestrial or otherwise, at their home anymore and that they could safely return. With some nervousness, they drove back and slowly entered the house. After an inspection, it did appear that they were once again alone.

The family slowly settled down and began to get ready for bed. As with all good horror movies, though, there is always one final scare. A female member of the family had just turned off the light in her room when she noticed an ominous silver glow coming from outside her bedroom window. Slowly, a clawed hand reached up from below and dragged its pointy fingers across the glass. She screamed; Elmer burst in and (you guessed it) shot the window out.

The goblins were spotted several more times that night, but it seemed that when the sun came up the ordeal was finally over.

The story quickly became big news. As time went on and saucer fans, ufologists, and sceptics continued to turn up at their home, the Sutton family got increasingly frustrated with the influx of unwanted visitors. Eventually, they put up a "No Trespassing" sign, but this did little to dissuade those turning up. Brave of these tourists to continue visiting, as it was well publicised how well armed the family was during the goblin attack.

The Suttons, realising that people were going to continue turning up no matter what, decided they might as well make a few bucks out of it. Sadly, this proved to be their undoing. They began charging visitors to enter their land, to ask the family questions, and to take pictures. As soon as word of this got out, many who believed their story quickly flipped and accused them of fabricating the whole thing in order to make some money. Not long after, the Suttons moved out.

When it comes to debunking what happened at the farmhouse that night, many sceptics simply paint the Sutton family and their friends as stereotypical hillbillies wasted on moonshine and shooting at drunken hallucinations.

While this isn't a stretch of the imagination to believe, their rural home without even the luxury of indoor plumbing certainly fit the stereotype, it isn't exactly true. Alcohol of any type was banned in the Sutton home by Glennie, the mother of Elmer. Apparently Glennie was so straight edge that if she even suspected that anyone in the house had been drinking, there would be "hell to pay" - What a buzzkill! This is backed up by Greenwell who said that everyone who turned up to the station that night was sober, and that he and his officers found no alcohol in the house.

While those involved in the Hopkinsville invasion may not have been brain scientists or rocket surgeons, they were all able to coherently describe what had happened and all their stories matched up. Even as time passed, their stories remained the same. Even when reporters started turning up and grilling the Suttons for information, they stayed true to their story. After a while, it seemed they wanted to just forget about the whole thing.

So if the Suttons weren't simply uneducated drunken hicks shooting at nothing, what were they blasting at that night?

Sceptics have claimed that the most likely suspect is a great horned owl. This species of owl is large, has big pointy ears, talons, and its eyes could easily glow if light hit them. It is said that those in the farmhouse that night simply confused a great horned owl or two for a militia of glow-in-the-dark space goblins.

Those who believe that something truly strange did happen that night argue against this theory. They say that the people involved would be familiar with owl species, Great Horned and otherwise, from their lives lived out in the country. It doesn't make sense that all involved would misidentify an owl to such a great extent that they would open fire on it for several hours. Also, wouldn't the constant sound of gunfire scare most wildlife away? This explanation also doesn't explain the glowing, the UFO, or why they would be attacking the house.

If the people involved weren't drunk and/or shooting at owls, we're left with the possibility that they did encounter something unusual, but what?

The UFO spotted by Billy Ray makes it easy to point towards the small creatures being extraterrestrial, and this is the most common theory, but what did they want? Elmer and Billy Ray certainly thought the first glowing humanoid they saw was playing out the traditional fantasy goblin role of being evil and opened fire on it, but is this the case? As it approached, it held its arms up in what could have been a sign of "Don't shoot!" or even the alien cliche of "We come in peace!" A sign that was ignored.

As the creatures continued to show up, were they simply trying to get a moment of the family's attention, but just kept getting shot at? Could they have wanted to communicate, to relay a message to the people of Earth, through this family? Was the goblin assault on the farmhouse not an assault at all, but just an attempt to make contact that a scared and heavily-armed family misinterpreted? Maybe these silver goblins were a more peaceful posse than their evil green relatives from fantasy media.

Sadly in many encounters with the unknown, the instant human reaction is to run, kill, or stand dumbfounded. Perhaps if we could shake or ignore this instinct we'd have a far greater knowledge of the paranormal and the supernatural.

Due to how crazy this story was and how outlandish and unique the description of the creatures was, the Hopkinsville Goblins case has become a classic in ufology and has even impacted mainstream media. The story inspired the terrifying found-footage film *Alien Abduction: Incident in Lake County* and the more family-friendly *E.T. the Extra-Terrestrial*. The description of the goblins appropriately influenced the design of a creature called a Hobkins Gremlin in the tabletop roleplaying game *Pathfinder*. The creators of the game had obviously done their homework, as they gave this creature the ability to levitate.

Perhaps the most important thing this case gave to pop culture though was a phrase. A phrase that these days seems quite dated, and is usually used as a term of endearment by those in ufology or in a derogatory manner by those opposed to the whole thing. A phrase that was used before the Hopkinsville

Goblins incident, but was popularised by it and forever associated with it afterwards. A phrase that honestly doesn't even really make much sense.

At the time, those involved referred to the creatures as "little silver men". This didn't have a very good ring to it though. The newspapers reporting the story employed a little bit of creative licence and dubbed the weird glowing goblin creatures from outer space "Little Green Men", and the rest is history.

BRAXXIE: THE FLATWOODS MONSTER

Nothing helps tourism quite like a monster.

Whether it's Loch Ness and its museum, boat tours, and souvenirs built around Nessie, Point Pleasant with its chrome statue in the likeness of Mothman and yearly festival dedicated to the cryptid, South Jersey with its nature walks and guided hikes that take you right through the forest where many have encountered a flying devil with hooved feet, you can bet that if a place has been home to a strange encounter, they'll let the world know about it. And why not?

These encounters, when looked back on, can be interesting, entertaining, and fun. At the time, though, they can be anything but. Nessie witnesses have been terrified when spotting a humongous beast straight out of the Jurassic age emerging from the loch, Mothman petrified locals with his ten-foot wingspan and glowing red eyes, the people who encountered a winged creature in the South Jersey Pine Barrens were traumatised by seeing something that belonged in folklore.

The town of Flatwoods in Braxton County, West Virginia has its own mini-tourism industry built around a bizarre and terrifying encounter with an unknown entity.

At just after 7.00 PM on September 12, 1952, three young boys — brothers Fred and Edward May and their friend Tommy Hyer — were out playing near their school when they saw something strange in the darkening sky. They saw a pulsing red light cross the heavens and land behind a hill on the property of a nearby farmer, G. Bailey Fisher. The boys were understandably surprised to see such a sight. They had to tell someone, but who? At the age they were, there was only one authority figure that reigned above all others, and it wasn't the police or the military.

They all went to the home of the May brothers and told the boys' mother what they had seen. "A flying saucer?" they thought, "Mum'll know what to do!" Kathleen May listened to the boys, but was sure it was just their imaginations. The kids insisted over and over that they had seen something descend from the sky and land close by. They pleaded with her to go and check what they were sure was still on the Fisher farm. It had been a long day, it was getting late, and she couldn't really be bothered to go and chase imaginary martians with the boys, but she was starting to realise how serious they were. Eventually, they managed to wear her down and she relented. "Okay," she told the three, "Let's go have a look."

As it was now getting quite dark, she reasoned she should probably take an escort for herself and the kids. Mrs May knocked on the door of their seventeen-year-old neighbour, Gene Lemon. Lemon was a National Guardsman, so in the unlikely event that there actually *was* something out there over the hill, he'd be able to employ his in-depth military training to defend and protect the woman and children. Besides, Lemon owned a flashlight which would probably come in handy. Mrs May told Lemon the story that the kids had told her and of course he agreed to come along. Who could ever pass up a UFO hunt?

Mrs May, Lemon, the three young UFO witnesses, and two more kids who had taken an interest in this impromptu trip to the nearby farm headed towards the alleged landing site.

As this group started walking towards the Fisher farm, Lemon's dog Richie ran ahead of them. He went up and over the hill, out of sight. They heard Richie barking, then he went quiet. Seconds later Richie came running back to them terrified, his tail literally between his legs. What had the dog so scared? As they approached the top of the hill themselves, they could see a red glow coming from the other side.

When they reached the top of the hill and looked over, they saw that the red glow was coming from a strange craft roughly fifty feet away. The craft was described as looking like a pulsing ball of fire. As it pulsed, a thumping sound could be heard. They got closer to the craft and noticed a mist hanging in the air that stung their eyes and noses.

Just as they were coming to terms with what they were looking at, Gene Lemon noticed something to the left of the pulsing object. He saw two green glowing lights in amongst some foliage, which he assumed were the eyes of an animal. He quickly shone his flashlight in the direction of these eyes and revealed something far more shocking than any nocturnal critter.

What the group saw illuminated by Gene's flashlight was a ten-foot-tall, semi-humanoid figure. Whatever it was, it seemed to be wearing a suit of some kind that covered its entire body, giving it more of a robotic or mechanical look than a biological one. Its head (or at least the helmet of the suit) was round and red, with two large glowing green eyes in the centre of it. Behind the head was a large cowl or hood that pointed upwards at the top. Its body was a dark green or black, and looked metallic. No legs were visible, and the body continued to flow down giving the creature the appearance that it was wearing a metal dress. Its arms were thin and skeletal. The hands were skinny and clawed. The creature seemed to be producing the mist, and also a foul odour, that was later described as smelling like sulphur.

Moments after the light hit the figure, the strange creature let out a hissing noise and moved towards the group. It was then they noticed that the creature had no feet and appeared to be hovering above the ground. The creature darted towards them before changing direction and heading back towards the pulsing red craft. It was at this point that the group fled the area as quickly as humanly possible. They ran back to the May home, and, after getting the biggest "We told ya so!" from the boys, Mrs May phoned the police and the local newspaper. As is the case in most reports of UFOs and aliens, the newspaper was on the scene before the authorities.

A reporter, Lee Steward Jr., arrived at the house sharpish and found Mrs May tending to some small cuts and bruises that the kids had received in their panicked fleeing of the Fisher farm. He found it difficult to get the story of what happened out of the group initially, as all were too shaken up to properly tell him what they had seen. As the night went on, Steward was eventually able to get the whole story of what happened earlier that night. After some more time, he was even able to convince Lemon to return with him to where they had seen the craft and creature.

As Steward and Lemon made their way back over the hill onto the Fisher farm, Lemon was relieved to find there was no more red glowing spaceship or robotic extraterrestrial. There was, however, some evidence left that backed up the group's story. A mist still blanketed the area and there was a terrible stench hanging in the air. A stench that Lemon and the group did not involuntarily create when they saw the creature.

The sulphur-like odour that the group had described coming from the creature remained, and Steward described it as "sickening and irritating", going on to add that it smelled like no other gas he had ever encountered, even during his time in the military. They found no other evidence of the creature or the craft in the misty darkness. It seemed like the Flatwoods Monster had gotten back into its ship and taken off, leaving little solid evidence that it was ever actually there in the first place. The next night, though, the monster was to return.

Roughly twenty miles south of Flatwoods, near Strange Creek (a fitting name) outside of Frametown, a couple were driving with their infant son on a quiet road between counties when their car suddenly, and seemingly without reason, died. Despite the man's best efforts, he could not get it to start again. The wife implied the problem may have been the husband's mechanic skills, but he debated this. Either way, it seemed like they were going nowhere for the foreseeable future.

The couple discussed what they could do. They had seen no other vehicles while they were driving on this road, and none had passed them since they had broken down, so flagging down a friendly motorist for help seemed out of the question. The area was unfamiliar to them, so they were unsure if there were any houses nearby where they could ask nicely to use a phone. Maybe one of them could go walking through the dark night in search of help? It wasn't an appealing thought. As they were talking, they noticed an intensifying smell of sulphur in the air. At first they blamed the baby, but the smell was even worse than a soiled diaper.

As the smell reached its most unbearable, the darkness in front of the car was suddenly illuminated in bright light. Revealed to the couple, hovering above the road mere feet ahead of the vehicle, was a ten-foot-tall humanoid. Their description of the creature matched what witnesses had told Steward the previous night. Or at least, from the waist down it did. It still had some sort of metal suit on, but its upper body was now revealed. Gone was the upper half of the metallic suit, red helmet and cowl. Revealed now was a bony and reptile-like body, and an equally reptilian head and face. The creature reportedly dragged its daggered claws over the hood of the car, then drifted away into the woods by the roadside.

As soon as the creature had hovered away and out of sight, the couple's car miraculously restarted and they got out of the area as quickly as they could and drove until they hit civilization, worried the floating lizardman could return at any second.

This creature became known as the Frametown Monster, and is widely believed to be the same creature as the Flatwoods Monster.

The stories of the monster in Flatwoods and Frametown are the two most well known encounters with the entity that seemed to arrive from outer space, but in the years that followed more stories emerged. When these two original encounters became public knowledge, it didn't take long before members of the Civilian Saucer Intelligence (the original CSI) arrived in Flatwood. In their investigations they unearthed some more interesting information from locals.

They interviewed the mother of a farmer who lived near where the original sighting took place. She claimed that around the same time that the children saw the UFO land that she felt her house shake and her radio cut out for almost an hour. They interviewed the director of the Board of Education, and he told them that he saw a UFO taking off the morning after the first encounter. They spoke to a mother that claimed to have seen the creature a week *before* the encounter on the farm. She claims to have seen it with her twenty-one-year-old daughter, and the mist and sulphur smell it produced had hospitalised the daughter for three whole weeks. Another story of seeing the Flatwoods Monster before the kids on the farm came from a woman named Mrs Harper.

Mrs Harper claims that a few days before the initial encounter she and some friends had been walking through the woods close to her home, roughly five miles away from Flatwoods. On the top of a nearby hill they saw a ball of fire. They didn't think much of it at the time, assuming it was just neighbours burning stuff. After they walked on a bit and looked back, though, they were surprised to see that the fire was gone. In its place now stood the silhouette of an impossibly tall man who seemed to be looking down at them. Mrs Harper and her friends were so shaken by this sight that they ran the rest of the way to their destination. After hearing about the Flatwoods Monster, Mrs Harper was convinced that she saw the same creature on the hill that day.

Although new information and sightings were discovered, it seemed that the monster had disappeared for good after scaring the couple in their car on the evening of September 13 1952.

So what exactly was this creature? Although the Flatwoods Monster is commonly referred to as a cryptid, it being an extraterrestrial is perhaps more possible. As the creature was seen next to a landed UFO, and although no one actually saw it enter or leave the craft, it doesn't take a huge leap of the imagination to reason that the creature was piloting it.

But why had it chosen to land on the Fisher farm? One theory suggests that the landing was not intentional, but was more of a crash. Some suggest that the red light that the boys saw in the sky was not a light attached to the craft, but a fire that had broken out on the hull of the UFO due to some unknown damage it had sustained.

If this is the case, then where did the UFO and the Flatwoods Monster go after the initial sighting over the hill? After the monster had deterred the makeshift investigators with its irritating mist and scared them all the way back to their house, was it able to repair its craft and get back into the stratosphere before Steward came to do his investigative journalism later that night? If the man from the local Board of Education is to be believed, the UFO didn't take off until the next morning.

Then there is the story of the couple in the car encountering the creature in a greater state of undress the next night. Is it possible that the Flatwoods Monster was able to fix its craft, but to the extent that it just barely worked, and was only able to move it to a more hidden location? Perhaps it was able to hover into some brush not too far from the site of the first encounter. Perhaps it was just a stone's throw away while Steward was back investigating that night. The next morning maybe the creature used whatever remaining fuel cells were left in the craft, put all power to the engines, and flew a greater distance away (explaining what the Board of Education director saw) to a location near Strange Creek.

Perhaps while the creature either attempted to repair its UFO, or waited for an intergalactic AA, it was stumbled upon by a couple driving through the area. Why was the Flatwoods Monster not in its full metal suit in this encounter? We've all seen the Diet Coke adverts where a hunky guy is working on his car, gets too hot, and takes his shirt off. Maybe the monster had the same idea, though its reptilian body and lizardman head had women screaming for an entirely different reason than in the ads.

We are left with a handful of stories that claim to have seen the creature prior to the encounter on the Fisher farm however. Possibly the Flatwoods Monster had been visiting the area for unknown reasons, but its landing on September 12 was more of an unplanned stop and stay.

Sceptics have explained what the kids saw in the sky that night as a meteor or aircraft. While the speed of the object seems to discount the plane hypothesis, a meteor could be possible. It is even within the realms of possibility that a meteor could fall from the sky and land on a local farm. It is the creature itself that sceptics have a harder time explaining.

The commonly accepted explanation is that Mrs May, Lemon, and the kids saw an owl. Some believe that what Lemon shone his flashlight on that night was nothing more than a barn owl sitting in a tree. They believe that the head shape and glowing eyes could easily have been an owl, while the body was simply the branches below that formed a kind of humanoid figure with thin arms and clawed hands. It seems unlikely that all seven people would confuse an owl for an extraterrestrial creature in a robotic suit, though. And it doesn't explain the landed craft nearby. It also doesn't explain the encounter near Strange Creek the next night, or the stories that the CSI later unearthed.

There is of course the possibility that everyone involved was just making the whole thing up. The first seven to encounter the Flatwoods Monster were reportedly badly shaken, something that would be hard to fake unless they'd been taking acting classes. They also had matching stories which they never changed, speaking to their sincerity. There is also no evidence to suggest that the couple in the car the next night had heard about this initial encounter. It seems almost impossible that they could make up a description of a creature that was so unusual but also coincidentally very similar to one seen just twenty-four hours before.

While some of the stories that were discovered later could feasibly have come from people who got caught up in monster hysteria, or just wanted to be part of the story, the two original encounters in Flatwoods and Frametown remain very hard to explain. It seems that these people did indeed experience something very strange. Something that cannot be explained away by the simple misidentification of an owl.

In the years since, the Flatwoods Monster has become something of a mascot for the town. Despite the initial terror it caused by appearing to these locals, much like Nessie, Mothman, and the Jersey Devil, the Flatwoods Monster has very much become a tourism monster. Just like Mothman, the monster has its own museum which houses items from the initial encounters and shares the stories with visitors. You can also buy yourself Flatwoods Monster t-shirts, caps, figurines, and more in the giftshop. Around the town, five large chairs have been placed which have been built in the likeness of the monster. If you get yourself photographed sitting in all five, the town's visitor bureau gives you a sticker. Very fun stuff! The Flatwoods Monster has even been given a cuter nickname; Braxxie, named for Braxton County where Flatwoods resides.

Interestingly, Braxxie has not stayed a mere local legend but has broken out into mainstream pop culture. Clearly the monster's iconic description was too good to waste. In the classic Nintendo 64 video game *The Legend of Zelda: Majora's Mask* certain enemies attacking a ranch, referred to only as "Them" or "They" in the game, are nearly identical to the Flatwoods Monster. If you fail to save the ranch from the invading Braxxie lookalikes, they abduct all the cows in classic alien fashion. If you manage to deter the invaders, you're rewarded with some milk. How generous!

Outside of video games, the monster has been featured in countless TV shows and specials about UFOs, unexplained mysteries, the supernatural, and the paranormal. Perhaps it was the original sketch of the monster, made in 1952 and based on the first eyewitness accounts, that made it so popular. It was certainly like nothing ever seen before or since. It was too out of this world and too bizarre for anyone to have just made up for a quick story.

Whatever the Flatwoods Monster was, whether it was an ET or an interdimensional entity in a mechanical suit (it wouldn't be the only one in this book), or even if you do think it was just people getting scared by an owl, there's no denying the story has gone down in history. The description of Braxxie has become iconic and has inspired a wealth of fantastic art based on the witnesses' descriptions.

Flatwoods, and all of Braxton County, has benefitted from the strange encounters in September 1952 and have created a mascot in the shape of a bizarre mechano-suited alien, and a whole tourism industry has been built around it. Sure, maybe the Flatwoods Monster terrified some locals and irritated a few eyes and noses at the time, but I think we can agree that in the long run it did more good than bad. And who knows, maybe that was Braxxie's intention all along.

THE NOT-SO-LITTLE GREEN MAN

As we know, the Hopkinsville Goblins were the first seemingly extraterrestrial creatures to popularise the term Little Green Men. But they were given this name incorrectly. They were silver, not green. But that isn't to say that green beings of otherworldly origin haven't been reported. One such being was seen in Europe in the mid-70s. Though calling this being a "Little Green Man" would also be incorrect. It was green, and it was humanoid, but it couldn't possibly be called little. This creature was in excess of nine feet in height. And honestly, that might have been the *least* weird thing about it!

Early in the morning of November 12, 1976, three men and a dog had a strange encounter on the grounds of a military airport base in Badajoz, Spain.

Two soldiers, José María Trejo and Juan Carrizosa Luján, were patrolling the grounds of Talavera la Real Air Base at around 1.45 AM. They were in the fuel storage area of the base, each in a different sentry box, when they suddenly heard a sound that they described as similar to radio interference. The interference sound then changed to a high pitched whistle that was so intense that it caused physical pain in the men's ears. This whistling sound went on for a full and annoying five minutes. José suspected something sinister was afoot, that the sound came from some sort of explosive device placed by a terrorist or saboteur, and asked Juan to help him inspect the area. They prepared their weapons, covered their ears, and began the search.

They thoroughly inspected the surrounding area while the whistle persisted. They could find no source of the sound but kept searching even after the noise had ceased. Strangely, the noise began a second time and lasted just as long as the first. Not long after the sound had stopped for the second time and the men were scratching their heads in confusion, they spotted an extremely bright light in the dark sky. It lasted for only fifteen seconds but made the soldiers even more confused about the situation.

At this point, another soldier turned up while doing his rounds with a guard dog. José and Juan explained to this third man what had been going on, and he and his dog decided to join them in searching the area. They found nothing in their initial search, but decided to report what had happened to the base's corporal. The corporal told the men to extend their search to the entire site.

After some time meticulously combing the grounds and sticking close to the wall that surrounded the base, they arrived at a sentry box that was still under construction close to a small wooded area. They heard the sound of footsteps and twigs snapping, and the guard dog took off into the treeline. Shortly after leaving, the dog returned to the men. It was visibly sick. The dog was staggering and seemed sluggish. The dog returned to the treeline several times, but its condition did not improve. Despite this, the dogs' military training kicked in. It began to circle the men, a technique it had been taught to protect its human co-workers. But protect them from what? The soldiers had seen no one else on the base. Apart from an annoying noise and a weird light in the sky, there had been nothing else out of the ordinary. The men shouted at the area they had heard the twigs snapping from, but received no response.

The soldiers and the dog planned to head back in the direction they came, performing a reverse sweep. It was while they were gearing up to turn and walk away that José got the feeling that someone was behind them. He spun around and, fifteen metres away from him, was something unexplainable emerging from the darkness.

What José, Juan, and the third soldier (and dog) saw was an exceptionally tall human-looking figure, at least three metres in height. It seemed to be made of a glowing green light that emanated from many pin pricks of brighter light on its body. The light was at its brightest along the edges of the creature, giving it the impression it had been highlighted or outlined. It was wearing a small helmet over its even smaller head. It had a broad barrel chest, overly long arms and legs that seemed not to fit its body, and no hands or feet.

José aimed his submachine gun at the tall glowing green creature, but couldn't pull the trigger. He felt stiff, and he physically couldn't move his limbs or (more importantly) his trigger finger. He fainted and fell to the ground. As José keeled over, it gave his friends the opportunity they needed. They had no problem firing their guns. They shot between forty and fifty rounds of ammunition into the creature of green light, but it seemed totally unaffected by the bullets. There was no sound of the bullets hitting the creature, though they were clearly going *into* it. The only sign that the creature even noticed that it was being shot like Al Pacino at the end of *Scarface* was that it kept glowing brighter and brighter. When it reached an apex of brightness, it vanished before the men's eyes. As the creature disappeared, the strange sound was heard by the men again, though it lasted only seconds this time.

With the glowing creature gone, the men quickly went to help José who was still on the ground. They got him to his feet and walked him back to the base to get medical help. The men told their superiors what had happened and the base was put on high alert. No one was sure exactly what the men had seen and shot at, but they couldn't risk this impossibly tall creature of glowing green energy sneaking around the base and messing with planes and flight equipment. No one on the grounds encountered it again.

When the sun came up, as many as fifty men went to inspect the area where the creature was seen. Curiously, there were no bullet casings from the forty to fifty shots fired to be found. There weren't even any bullet holes in anything in the surrounding area from missed shots or bullets that had gone straight through the glowing creature. This led some to think that the men had just made up their story of opening fire on an alien creature, but their guns were inspected by the Air Force and were found to have been fired. Though, what no one could decide was, fired at *what?*

The creature had disappeared, but its effect on José remained. Though he recovered from his initial fainting spell, it happened again in the base a few days after the encounter. He was hospitalised and diagnosed with a "nervous mal-adjustment". He had problems with vision becoming dark and headaches. Whether this was just José's body's way of dealing with seeing a creature that couldn't possibly exist, or whether it was something the creature physically caused in humans who saw it, is unsure. It seemed to have a similar effect on the guard dog, but the two other human witnesses were unharmed. Is it possible that the creature's green glow is somehow toxic to humans or animals who get too close to it? It wouldn't be the only unexplainable being to have these strange abilities (see Mothman and his conjunctivitis-causing eye beams).

Some have said that the Badajoz Creature was nothing more than a human intruder on the air base in a costume, but this theory ignores a lot of the facts. If this was the case, then was the unfindable high-pitched sound and the light in the sky also part of the intruder's plan, or just a coincidence? And how did the intruder make the costume? By standing on stilts and covering himself in glow-in-the-dark fabric? And how did he survive the barrage of gunshots? Was the glowing fabric also bullet proof? How did he disappear? Did he return to collect the casings from the bullets shot at him afterwards? And, most importantly, why would someone do all this? What would be the reason, motivation, or end goal? It almost seems more implausible that the Badajoz Creature *was* a human intruder.

So if it wasn't a regular person sneaking onto an air base in an impressive glow-in-the-dark Halloween costume who somehow survived getting riddled with bullets, what was it? The common theory is that it was an extraterrestrial, and it's easy to see why. While this may be the case, it may not be totally accurate. The Badajoz Creature may have been an alien, but maybe not a physical presence of an alien. Is it possible that it was a hologram or a projection of an alien? Could the high-pitched noise have been the sound of the projection taking form on Earth (and vanishing), beamed down from a ship far above? Possibly the light in the sky that the men saw? Was the glowing green just the colour of the projection? Was the helmet it wore on its small head how the creature saw through its hologram self, like the Oculus headsets we use to play virtual reality video games on Earth? Did the bullets cause no harm because the bullets weren't hitting anything physical? Were the bullets just absorbed by whatever advanced extraterrestrial substance made up the hologram? Did this substance also cause sickness in anyone or anything that got too close to it, almost like it was radioactive?

If an alien did project a hologram of itself onto an air base in Spain, what would its goal be? UFOs are commonly reported around areas that are making huge technological advancements. Was there possibly some secret project on the base that this alien race wanted to get a closer look at? It certainly did have a large security presence.

Perhaps if we knew more about the internal workings of this air base at the time period we could piece together what interest an alien race may have had in it.

ALBERT BENDER & THE MEN IN BLACK; A VILLAINOUS ORIGIN STORY

Y ou'd be forgiven for assuming that the Men in Black are nothing more than a Hollywood blockbuster movie franchise with increasingly terrible instalments.

You'd also be forgiven, when told that the Men in Black are very much real, for believing that they are the good guys. In the previously mentioned film series, the MIB are the defenders of Earth from alien menace, and they can sing a catchy song about it too. The reality of the MIB is quite different. While some do believe that the Men in Black are on our side, or at the very least are a government organisation of some kind, there are far more who view them as something more sinister.

Those who believe that the MIB are at the very least human, believe they are working to silence and intimidate those who have seen UFOs and extraterrestrials and those who research them. They believe the MIB work in secret with the governments of the world to keep information and interest in visitors from other planets underwraps for our own protection or for the interests of those in charge.

There is a whole other side to the MIB theory though. One that views them as something other than human. Due to the strange appearance and seemingly supernatural abilities they possess, many have theorised that the MIB are more than shady government agents trying to creep out people who write about UFOs. Theories range from the MIB being alien in origin themselves, and extend to them being interdimensional beings, ghosts, demons, and even time travellers. As outlandish as these more paranormal theories may sound, the idea of a team of supernatural entities clad in black suits became a reality for one unsuspecting ufologist in the 1950s.

Albert Bender was, depending on your point of view, one of the coolest or one of the weirdest people of the time.

In 1952, Bender founded the International Flying Saucer Bureau (the IFSB for short), following a fascination with UFOs that had lasted years. As if forming one the first civilian UFO investigation groups wasn't enough to give people a strong opinion of him, Albert was also obsessed with horror movies, science fiction, the paranormal, the occult, and witchcraft.

He decorated the attic room in his step-father's house, where he lived and operated the IFSB out of, with creepy faces that he painted on the walls and Halloween decorations like fake skulls and plastic spiders. He began to refer to his living space as his "Chamber of Horrors", and if anyone dared come to visit his DIY haunted house he had a horror movie sound effects LP loaded up on his record player to really set the mood. As you can imagine, he was a big hit with the ladies.

While skulking around his intentionally spooky attic room like a bootleg Doctor Frankenstein, Bender worked tirelessly on his beloved IFSB. He published UFO stories and reports in a series of magazines and newsletters, and it was quickly becoming a huge success. His dream of setting up a worldwide community of UFO investigators who all worked together and shared their reports was becoming a reality. Membership of the IFSB was expanding exponentially. The IFSB seemed like it would become the group to join for anyone interested in the truth behind the flying saucer phenomenon. Then, in September of 1953, it was all over. Bender announced in his magazine *Space Review* that not only was he shutting the IFSB down, he was quitting the field of ufology altogether.

Readers of *Space Review* and members of IFSB were shocked. "Why would a man with such an intense interest and fascination in UFOs suddenly just quit?" they thought. His sign-off did nothing to answer their questions and served only to increase speculation. In the final issue Bender wrote that "The mystery of flying saucers are no longer a mystery" and went on to say that UFO information was being kept from the public by a higher source. He then advised that anyone involved in saucer work to be very cautious.

People were baffled, and theories as to what had happened to Bender started to fly wild. What he wrote seemed to suggest that he had learnt *something* about UFOs but was unable to share it with his fellow saucer fans. It also seemed like he was warning these same people that their research could prove dangerous. Had Bender's own research taken him down a dark path? Just what had happened to Albert Bender?

The downfall of the IFSB was put into motion one night in July 1952 by the simple ringing of a telephone. Bender could hear the house phone from his spooky attic room, but no one answered it. He reasoned that his stepfather must have gone out and resolved to do the annoying task himself.

He descended the stairs and scooped up the ringing phone. "Hello?" said Bender, but no answer came. He said it again, but still no response. Bender was sure that someone was on the other end of the phone, but they were refusing to speak. Just as he was starting to get irritated, he was suddenly struck by a tremendous headache. The pain was so instant and severe that he hung up the phone and quickly went back to his room to rest. A phantom migraine over the phone was strange, but things were about to get stranger.

A couple of days later, when Bender was feeling better, he decided to head out to the cinema to take in a movie. It was what happened afterwards that was truly cinematic though. As Bender made his way back home that night after the film, he became sure he was being followed. Someone was stalking him, staying out of sight and hidden in the shadows and darkness of the eerily quiet city streets. He repeatedly looked back and could see no one, but his paranoia remained. He got back to his (stepfather's) house as quickly as he could, got inside, and locked the door. He was safe. Or so he thought.

He headed back to his Chamber of Horrors but stopped before heading inside. From under the crack at the bottom of the door, he could see a glow coming from inside his room. He hadn't left the light on when he went out earlier; he was sure of it. He was confused but reasoned that his stepdad had possibly gone in to get something (a fake skull maybe), though he knew the man was likely already asleep in his own room.

Bender opened the door and was baffled by what he saw. The light seen under the door wasn't coming from any bulb. Levitating in the centre of his room was a glowing ball. He was also assaulted nasally by an extremely strong smell of sulphur. The glow from the object began to hurt his eyes almost instantly, and he reached for the lightswitch. He flicked on the bedroom lights, and the strange object was gone. Confused, he searched his room. Bender quickly realised that certain files, notes and research on UFOs were moved and out of order. It seemed that the ball had been thumbing through his IFSB papers.

Later, in November 1952, Bender returned to the cinema. Hopefully he had one of those unlimited film passes or these tickets would be costing him a lot, and writing about UFOs doesn't pay much (trust me).

As he watched the movie on the big screen that night, he began to feel unusual. He felt intense feelings of dread, anxiety and terror all mixed together into one terrible mental cocktail. As these feelings steadily increased and the cocktail got stronger, Bender saw something unexplainable in the periphery of his vision. In a seat just a few away from his own, he saw a man suddenly appear.

The man was well dressed, wearing a black suit and a homburg hat. Perhaps Bender could have ignored this fashionable man who suddenly and mysteriously appeared near him, if it wasn't for his eyes. This Man in Black had eyes that glowed with the intensity of flashlights. Bender was once again hit with a sudden headache, just like when he answered the phone. He knew this was no coincidence; it was the man who now sat with him in the theatre that had called and psychically attacked him with a migraine, and now he was back for round two! He closed his eyes and tried to fight against the pain and the stomach-churning sickness that the ache in his skull caused.

When he opened his eyes again, he was relieved to see that the black-suited man had vanished as quickly as he had appeared. Bender turned back to the screen and tried to watch the movie, but his head ached too badly. A few more minutes passed, then Bender felt the feeling of being watched, just like he had on the city streets. He looked over, and in the aisle he saw the same MIB again. This time his glowing eyes were fixed directly on Bender. Could it just have been a snappy-dressed theatre usher staring daggers of white hot hatred at him for dropping some popcorn that he'd have to clean up after the performance? It seemed unlikely. Deciding that enough was enough, he quickly left the cinema without seeing the conclusion of the film or asking for a refund.

Over the next few months, Bender continued to see men in black suits that appeared and disappeared in the periphery of his vision. His headaches continued, some lasting for days and days. The smell of sulphur returned to his attic room and no cause could be found. Bender even started to experience poltergeist activity in his home. These strange phenomena seemed to increase in intensity, as if building towards something. And building towards something they were. In August 1953, Albert Bender had a visit that would go down in ufology history. A visit that would begin the legend of the Men in Black.

Although Bender kept the details of the visit that caused him to abandon his UFO research secret, elements of it did start to leak out. Bender told a close friend (though it took much questioning and Bender still remained fairly vague) and fellow ufologist who was also a member of the IFSB, who then told Gray Barker (as an interesting sidenote; Barker was one of the first to research The Flatwoods Monster). Barker later wrote about the Men in Black in the fantastically titled book *They Knew Too Much About Flying Saucers*. A title I can certainly relate to.

The story goes that Bender was in his Chamber of Horrors working on the next issue of *Space Review* when he heard a knock on the door. He sighed, put his papers to the side, and descended from his attic to see who was outside. To his surprise, three black-suited men stood at his front door. Men that looked fairly familiar to Bender by this point. Were these the same men he'd been seeing appearing and disappearing at will?

One of the men held a letter. A letter that Bender had sent earlier. Bender said that the letter contained information on flying saucers. He had had a breakthrough and wrote down some new theories on what these craft could be. He sent this information to a friend to get their opinion, but that letter would never arrive. Somehow these men knew what Bender had written to his friend, and had intercepted it. They then invited themselves in.

In Bender's office/attic, two of the men spoke while the other one stayed silent. They told Bender that the government knew what flying saucers were. They told him that the smartest men in the country were working on a defence for them, but couldn't find an answer. They told him that he should stop his research if he valued his freedom.

These men seemed more like government agents than the man with the glowing eyes from the cinema; the mention of having great thinkers working on the UFO problem and the vague threats of having him arrested also gave this impression, but something still wasn't quite right about them. They behaved oddly, rifling through his IFSB papers with seemingly no purpose. They showed particular interest in a map on Bender's wall. The mute man stared intensely at Bender, as if trying to hypnotise him. Had the creepy guys in black suits he'd been seeing in the corner of his vision adopted a more official form to get their point across?

Bender hinted that the men told him the truth behind the UFO phenomenon, but he would not share it. Whatever he had written in the letter that these men had intercepted may have had the definite answer, or close to it. Had Bender cracked the secret of Unidentified Flying Objects almost accidentally?

The men then told him that he would disband his UFO group, stop publishing his magazine, and destroy his research if he knew what was good for him. They confiscated some papers, research, the IFSB membership list, and back issues of *Space Review*, then went on their unmerry way.

As Bender was quite vague on his visit; some have added more fantastical elements to the story. There was just enough left up to interpretation that people could add or imply whatever they wanted to fit their idea of what the MIB were or are. Whether they believed they were shady agents, aliens themselves, demons from the underworld, or anything else, there was room in this story for it all.

Perhaps the vaguest of all was the start of the story. Due to the lack of information regarding *how* the MIB arrived at Bender's abode, some versions of this story have extrapolated that the MIB did not knock at his front door at all, but that they somehow just appeared in his attic room. This version is obviously much more creepy and supernatural, and is something that Bender would later build on in his later retelling of this story (we'll get to that version here in a second).

However they arrived, and whatever actually happened in the attic room, though, after their visit, Bender became quite ill and was unable to eat for several days. Convinced that these Men in Black would make good on their threats, Albert Bender quit the UFO scene.

Or, at least, he did for a little while. In 1962, Bender released the book *Flying Saucers and The Three Men* in which he discussed his experiences researching UFOs and his encounters with the MIB; the titular *Three Men*. The book read as something of a retelling of the events covered in Gray Barker's *They Knew Too Much* which came out in 1956 and also covers Bender's MIB troubles, but from a different perspective.

Barker's book contained a more subdued version of what happened when Albert was visited by the trio of black-suited men and omitted most of the more supernatural elements, and didn't include the phone calls, glowing balls, or cinema sightings. Barker's version of Bender's story seemed to lean more into the theory that the Men in Black were government agents of some sort. Sure, they were weird and a little spooky, but they were probably just regular guys (probably). Whether you believed they were human or otherwise, this version of events is what really set the groundwork for most MIB encounters that followed and cemented the Men in Black as the boogeymen that would keep ufologists awake at night, hiding under their covers and cuddling their precious research for protection.

In Bender's book, though, his new version of what happened that August night took a more psychedelic turn. It kicks off much the same way; Bender was working on *Space Review* in his attic late one night, when his eyes beheld an eerie sight. Suddenly, three black-suited men were with him in his Chamber of Horrors. Three men that Bender described as looking like priests. They wore black suits, black shoes, black hats, black ties, and even black gloves. How they got in is unknown, but Bender's stepfather certainty didn't let them in. It seemed as if they just materialised in the room. To add to their supernatural presence, Bender described them as seeming to hover just above the floor. As if this wasn't enough proof that these Men in Black were something otherworldly, they chose to communicate telepathically.

The men quickly formed a circle around Bender to stop him from escaping. They then each placed a hand on him, and he passed out. When Bender awoke, he was shocked to discover that the MIB had teleported him to their secret base. A secret base that was unexpectedly located beneath the ice of Antarctica.

The men then informed Bender that they were indeed alien visitors, and shapeshifting ones at that. They explained that they were on Earth to extract some sort of substance from our seawater that they used as a power source. Possibly as the fuel that UFOs run on. It would be cheaper than petrol. They explained some more about their culture, religion, the fact that they hatched from eggs, and their home planet before warning Bender not to tell anymore about what he'd seen or what he'd been told. They told him that he may be tempted to share his experiences, and that when he felt this urge he would be subjected to horrible headaches.

They then teleported him back home, unsure of why he'd been given this information if he wasn't allowed to tell anybody. Bender was back in his chamber alone, though the MIB had left a foul-smelling yellow smoke in their wake.

Albert would later even claim at a UFO conference that the MIB had given him special abilities. Abilities not unlike the super powers you might see in a modern big budget blockbuster movie franchise. Since his trip to Antarctica, he had to only wish ill will on someone and they would get into an unfortunate accident or, in the case of a man who had the audacity to smoke a cigar near him on the bus, even die. I'm looking forward to the inevitable "Super Ufologist" graphic novel and subsequent film adaptation.

Bender would then disappear from saucerology again, this time permanently. Until the end of his life it seemed like he just wanted to forget about UFOs, aliens, and the Men in Black. At this point, who could blame him?

Bender's experience was not the first encounter with the Men in Black, but his was the one that really started the legend. After the MIB began harassing poor Albert in his attic room and at the cinema, the flood gates opened.

Ufologists began receiving intimidating visits from men wearing dark suits who encouraged them to abandon their research. But the MIB didn't stop at those interested in UFOs; regular people who had seen a strange craft in the sky and had never even heard of the infamous MIB began receiving visits too. These witnesses were told to forget about what they had seen and report it to no one.

To this day, the Men in Black continue to make their terrifying visits to those involved and associated with UFOs and the paranormal. Since Bender's initial encounter in 1952, they have only gotten weirder, not just in appearance but also in abilities. Just by reading this book, you've probably ended up on their radar (sorry, my bad).

Was Albert Bender harassed by strange men in black suits as a result of his UFO research? If we ignore his Pink Floyd music video style trip to Antarctica, is it possible that he was visited by Men in Black, just not the supernatural kind?

A common non-paranormal theory for the MIB is that they are simply government agents. There is evidence that the US government was interested in UFOs during the time period. In 1952, the same year as the IFSB was formed, Project Blue Book also came into existence. Project Blue Book was the codename for the study of UFOs, and was specifically set up by the US Air Force to try and debunk supposed sightings. It ran until 1969 and is famously associated with astronomer and professor J. Allen Hynek. Hynek came on as a sceptic, but over the course of his research became a believer in extraterrestrial intelligences.

Hynek would later develop the "Close Encounter Scale" which measured experiences with UFOs. The scale ranged from the mild seeing lights in the sky, to the extreme seeing a craft and its occupants; the latter being the famous 'Close Encounter of the Third Kind'. This type of encounter became the inspiration for the similarly titled Steven Spielberg film, in which Hynek acted as a consultant on and even had a small cameo in.

The reason for the government's interest in the growing saucer craze was likely less to do with a concern in visitors from another planet, and more likely a concern in advanced technology from an enemy of the country. If another nation was sending machines that were so advanced that witnesses believed they came from outer space, this would certainly be alarming to the military. If civilians were gathering information on these crafts, it makes sense that government agents would be sent out to get these reports so they could officially compile as much information as they could on them.

There is also the possibility that the UFOs were simply experimental aircraft from the US army. If these craft were meant to be kept top secret, it makes sense that agents would be sent to confiscate any information a civilian had on them. Especially if the civilian was sharing this information in an increasingly popular magazine.

If the Men in Black are just boring old humans, that doesn't mean that UFOs can't somehow be involved. It is believed by some that the wreckage from the supposed flying saucer crash at Roswell in 1947 was sent to Area 51 with the intention of finding out how it worked, and then building their own version of it. Could the Men in Black be government agents out confiscating information on reverse-engineered flying saucers?

While it is possible that government agents visited Bender, and government agents can certainly be blamed for some MIB encounters throughout ufology history, it doesn't explain their seemingly supernatural abilities. Bender describes them as having the ability to appear and disappear at will, being able to inflict pain psychically, and communicate telepathically. As the MIB have continued to harass and creep people out over the years they have shown these abilities again and again, often to people who have never heard of Albert Bender or his story prior to their own visit.

Although the MIB seemed fairly normal and human in appearance (apart from the glowing eyes), as encounters have continued they have occasionally taken on a weirder look. Some people have described them as being totally hairless, others have claimed they have no lips, others have said that their lips are painted on and have even smeared when touched, more have said that they have no fingernails or eyelids. Even their classic black suits have at points had additions. Sometimes they are described as wearing strange helmets, goggles, and masks.

If they are just humans working for some government agency dedicated to keeping UFOs underwraps, none of this makes sense. The only explanation would be if these agents arrive loaded with special effects and makeup, like they've just raided the *Industrial Light & Magic* warehouse.

If the Men in Black aren't just humans working a day job, then what are they? The answer may be in the realms of the paranormal.

Could the MIB be aliens themselves? They admitted to Bender that they were when they took him on his little field trip to Antarctica. Thankfully, this is not the only evidence. The MIB always turn up after (and sometimes before!) UFOs are seen in an area. Could they be more connected to flying saucers than we think? The Men in Black are commonly described as looking almost human, but not quite. Something always seems slightly off about them, whether it's the lack of hair, skin that doesn't look natural, or painted-on lips.

Could the MIB be aliens in disguise? Could alien beings be visiting UFO witnesses and researchers in bizarre human disguises to try and discourage them from sharing their stories so as to keep themselves underwraps? It would explain their connection to the UFO phenomena and their weird appearances and abilities. Perhaps Bender's trip to Antarctica was more of projected psychic vision, rather than an actual physical visit. Could they have given Bender this totally unbelievable experience in order to discredit his entire story and throw others off their foul-smelling scent?

Could they be beings from another dimension? Could they travel through dimensional wormholes in pursuit of other entities from various dimensions? Could they be some sort of extradimensional, rather than extraterrestrial, police force in pursuit of escapees from other realms? Could they be sent to return

UFOs to their proper dimension and silence those who have seen more than they should have? It would explain why the MIB have been known to show up after sightings of cryptids, if we believe that cryptids are also creatures from other dimensions.

The MIB were a constant presence in Point Pleasant during the Mothman's residency there. Could Mothman have slipped through a dimensional portal into the small West Virginia town? Were the MIB there to bring him home?

Could the Men in Black be time travellers? Some believe that they are indeed human, but a more evolved type of human from the far future. A future in which time travel has been invented. The belief is that criminals in the future travel back in time to change the timeline to benefit themselves. In this scenario, the MIB are the police force sent back to catch them. The weird appearance is due to humans looking quite different in several hundred thousand years. As for the suits, it's to help them fit in. What is the UFO connection? UFOs are time machines that these cops and robbers travel back in.

Do the MIB visit people who have seen these time travelling villains in order to stop them talking about what they've seen and protect the primary timeline before getting back into their own UFO, pushing it to eighty-eight miles per hour, and heading back to the future?

Could the Men in Black be demons? In old writings, demons, and even the devil himself, are described as appearing on Earth as tall men wearing all black. Albert Bender had an interest in the occult. Could he have summoned black-suited demons from the depths of Hell while performing some sort of ritual? Did they attach themselves to ufology due to the manner that they were summoned and who summoned them? Could Bender have inadvertently summoned the nemesis of ufologists?

Could Bender indeed have summoned the Men in Black, but could they have come not from the depths of Hell, but from the far reaches of outer space?

Bender would frequently try to project telepathic messages from his mind into space in the hopes of reaching a benevolent alien species and receiving some sort of reply. He believed in this astro-thought projection concept so much that he began to let his fellow ISFB members know when he would be attempting it, and encouraged them to join in. His belief was that if more people were thinking and projecting the same message, the stronger it would be.

Could Bender and pals' space-travelling message have been intercepted by the malevolent Men in Black before it reached the kindly extraterrestrials it was intended for? There is a theory that states that attempting to contact extraterrestrial beings is a bad move, as they will almost certainly be hostile towards us. Could the alien race we now know as the Men in Black have been blissfully unaware of humans and Earth until they got a strange message of peace and friendship on their psychic radar? Could Bender and his IFSB members, with the best of intentions, have painted a huge target on our planet for the whole universe to see?

A final theory is, of course, that Bender just made the whole thing up. Even people who believe his story to an extent tend to agree that his Antarctica trip was fabricated, perhaps to sell books. It's also possible that Bender hallucinated the whole thing. He had a history of mental illness and was believed to possibly have had epilepsy, which could explain the smells and headaches. He had OCD and was prone to bouts of intense paranoia. All of this (or even just some) combined could definitely have spawned the Men in Black in Bender's mind.

After he began speaking about them, the idea could have simply been adopted by fellow ufologists over the years and caused a case of extended mass hysteria in their own moments of paranoia. Is it possible that the Men in Black are simply a figment of people's imagination borne out of Bender's own story and their own deep-seated fears?

Sure it's possible, but as Kurt Cobain rasps on an underrated Nirvana classic; "Just because you're paranoid, don't mean they're not after you."

THE SWEDISH JELLY BLOBS

In the final episode of the first season of the original series of *Star Trek*, the crew of the *Enterprise* beam down to a planet to find its population terrorised by small alien jelly-like single cell organisms. It was a pretty good instalment, though the previous episode, the classic time-travelling hijinks-based "City on the Edge of Forever", really should have been the season finale.

Still, "Operation – Annihilate!" aired on April 13 1967, closing the first season of the greatest sci-fi show of all time. Unbeknownst to the cast, crew, and viewers of *Star Trek,* though, jelly aliens had already attacked nine years earlier. And they hadn't attacked a far off alien planet. They had struck in Sweden.

On December 20th, 1958, Hans Gustafsson and Stig Rydberg were driving from Höganäs to Heisenberg. It was very early in the morning, around 3.00 AM, and the road was obscured by a thick fog. Hans drove very slowly due to the lack of light and the obscured vision, fearing he may get into an accident if he picked up too much speed. As the men were travelling home after a night on the town, and had full bladders, it wasn't long before nature called. And when it called, they were still far from home. They had no choice; Hans pulled over.

He parked by the side of the road near the village of Domsten. This was the perfect area, as there was a nearby woods that would offer the men some privacy. They jumped out of the car, ran towards the woods, and... Well, I probably don't need to describe this next part.

After the men had dealt with the pressing matter at hand, they noticed that there was a light emanating from within the woods. They couldn't see what the light was coming from due to the fog, but there was definitely something in there. It changed colour and hue, so they reasoned it probably wasn't a flashlight or a lantern. Hans and Stig were struck with curiosity and, with nothing left to distract them, they decided to check it out. Wandering into unfamiliar dark and misty woods to investigate an unknown light source? Surely, they thought, nothing could go wrong!

As they headed into the woods they stopped by a sign that said camping was prohibited. They thought the light was maybe coming from people camping illegally (or campers who just hadn't seen the sign due to the fog). As they got closer to the light though, their accidental illegal camper theory came apart. As they came to a clearing in the trees, the men saw what looked like a parked flying saucer. It was roughly fifteen feet wide, three feet tall, and sat on three legs that were two feet long. It was disc shaped and seemed to shimmer with a changing coloured light; this was what the men had seen through the mist.

Before the men could process what they were seeing, they met the saucer's occupants. Suddenly, the UFO was surrounded by three-foot-long beings that resembled usually-microscopic single-celled organisms, dwarfing the inches-long aliens from the *Star Trek* episode. They were blue in colour and were described as moving around the saucer like large pieces of jelly. Despite having no eyes, the gelatin aliens saw Hans and Stig and attacked them.

The men were swarmed by the wobbly creatures before they could react. The beings stuck to Hans and Stig and enveloped their limbs into their jelly-like bodies. The men fought to free their arms and legs, but the creatures had them locked in their weirdly elastic bodies in a strange sort of grip. Once the jelly aliens had them where they wanted them, they started to drag the men towards their ship.

When they realised they were heading for a potential alien abduction, the men began to fight against their gelatinous assailants as hard as they possibly could. As soon as they managed to shake off one of the overgrown amoebas, though, another would leap on in its place. At one point Stig, in an act of primal frenzy, attempted to punch one of the creatures. His arm was simply absorbed into its body, up to his elbow. Stig began to worry that the creatures possessed some type of telepathic ability. They seemed able to predict and counter his every move, like psychic kung-fu masters.

After an epic struggle, Stig was able to free all of his enveloped limbs and made a run back through the woods towards the parked car. He glanced back and was horrified to see two of the jelly creatures chasing him. Perhaps more concerning was what he saw of his friend. Hans had evidently made it back through some of the woods too. He was now clinging to the "No Camping" sign with both hands while two blue bags of alien jelly tried to drag him back to the UFO by his legs.

Stig thought about helping his friend, but reasoned that it was hopeless. Hans watched as his friend ran past without giving him a second look. He thought he had been left to the mercy of sentient extraterrestrial jelly. But Stig had a plan.

Stig reached the parked car and dove back inside, slamming the door behind him to keep his protoplasmic pursuers at bay. He had just seconds to spare and one shot to make his plan work. It was a long shot but it was the only shot he had. He pressed on the horn with all his might. Then he pressed on it again, and again. For some reason, the loud sound of the car horn had some sort of adverse effect on the alien creatures. Whether it was audio vibration causing pain to their physical form, whether they thought Stig was signalling for help, or whether it was just a super annoying sound, the jelly beings were not a fan of it.

The two creatures that had been chasing Stig instantly turned and ran (if jelly can indeed run) at the piercing sound of the horn. The two that had been trying to tug Hans off (of the sign) dropped him to the ground and darted back towards their ship. Hans seized his freedom and ran back to the car, joining his friend. Just after Hans entered the vehicle, both men saw the strange shimmery ship taking off and disappearing into the night sky with a loud whistle. All that remained was the smell of the creatures, which Hans and Stig would later recount as smelling like ether and burnt sausages.

The men sat in the car in silence, each trying to process what they had just experienced. This was like nothing they had ever heard of before. What should they do? Report it? To whom? It took Hans twenty minutes before he was physically able to start the car and continue their drive to Heisenberg.

The men had yet to speak a word to each other and they travelled in total silence until they were safely within the limits in Heisenberg. When they spoke, they didn't discuss what had happened to them in the woods outside Domsten, they didn't try to make sense of the experience or find a logical explanation for it, they didn't even debate who would use the shower first to try and get the smell of ether and sausages off of them, they simply agreed that they should not tell a soul about what had happened that night.

Hans and Stig kept their encounter secret for three days, and may have kept it for their entire lives, but it was becoming obvious to those around them that something had happened to the two men. They were both experiencing intense insomnia, anxiety, and paranoia. Their physical injuries were also hard to ignore. They both had large bruises from where the jelly aliens had latched onto them. Both men had also developed inflamed eyes (a recurring theme after encountering strange creatures). They could both still hear the high pitched whistle of the UFO taking off ringing in their ears. Unfortunately, no matter how much they bathed and scrubbed, the stink of the alien jelly also remained on them.

On the third day, unable to keep their secret any longer, they told Hans' family what had happened to them that night. The family, cruelly, laughed at them. They continued with their story despite the laughter, showed their physical injuries and spoke about their mental ones. Soon the laughter died down as, one by one, the family realised that Hans and Stig were serious. The men were happy to have told their tale and, more importantly, to be believed. But this did not help with their feelings of anxiety or their inability to sleep. Hans' mother, Anna, decided that it would be a good idea to contact the local newspaper.

Anna likely thought that if the story got some publicity someone may step forward that could help her son and his friend, though more cynical people believe she did it to drum up business for her dry cleaning empire. Perhaps the plan was to eventually run an ad that claimed that her cleaning services were *so good* that she could even remove the stink of alien sausages from clothing.

Either way, their story was printed and it captured the imaginations of those who read it; including the local police. On the 9th of January 1959, Hans and Stig were asked to report to the police station in Heisenberg for questioning. Questioning that would end up lasting eleven hours.

Their interview with the authorities initially seemed to be geared towards discovering if a human enemy with advanced flying and jelly technology had invaded Swedish soil, then turned towards debunking the men's story as a hoax. They even tried the sneaky trick of leaving Hans and Stig in the room alone with a hidden microphone in hopes of catching them admitting their lie to each other. The men stuck to their story the whole time, whether in the room with officers or alone (with the hidden microphone).

After almost half a day in an interrogation room, the Heisenberg police accepted that the men weren't going to go back on their story, or slip up when re-telling it for the hundredth time. If the men weren't lying, they thought, maybe they were just insane. Hans and Stig were called back to the station to undergo a psychological evaluation and even hypnosis. After hours of tests and evaluations with mental health professionals, the men were found to be perfectly sane. In fact, those who evaluated them deemed that these men had indeed suffered some sort of traumatic incident, though they refused to cite ET jelly as the cause.

Despite the men showing no signs of lying and being judged to be within their right minds, the Swedish authorities still deemed the Domsten Blobs a hoax. A brief investigation was launched and the clearing where the men were attacked was searched, but a very slapdash job was done. According to Hans and Stig, the equipment used by the military in their investigation was inadequate and some of it didn't even work. It was easier for those in charge to simply say that the men had made the whole thing up, and for everyone to forget about it. It appeared that this conclusion had been reached before any real investigation had even been done.

Hans and Stig went back to their normal lives and the case faded into obscurity. The men were occasionally interviewed by ufologists, but it seemed as if there was no more information, clues, or leads to try and explain what the alien blobs were and what their business was in the woods outside of Domsten.

Here is where the case takes a turn; allegedly, at some point years after their intergalactic jelly attack, Hans, Stig, or both admitted their whole story was made up. They said the tale was inspired by the influx of sci-fi novels being released at the time, and, as the stretch of road outside of Domsten was said to be haunted, they decided it was the perfect setting for their own out-of-this-world adventure.

While this is information that can be found while researching the Domsten Blobs case, it's hard to find it as a direct quote from either man. It's usually cited to friends or acquaintances of the men that they had presumably confessed their hoax to. This quote seems to have originated some time in the 1980s, over twenty years after the blobs attacked. If the men did admit their attack was a lie, is it possible they just said this to try and put an end to twenty-plus years of questions about violent blue bags of jelly? After a few weeks, months, and years of "Hey, aren't you the alien jelly guy?" (or "Hej, är inte du den främmande gelékillen?" in Swedish according to Google Translate) I can imagine it would get quite tiresome.

After all, they initially didn't want to talk about it ever again. They stuck to their story through ridicule, police interrogation, and psychological evaluation. And not to mention the physical and mental damage the men endured. Could they just force themselves to stay awake for days? Did they just beat each other up to give themselves bruises, then claim the bruises came from semi-solid aliens enveloping their limbs and dragging them towards a parked UFO? And did they simply give each other pink-eye (the less said about how they'd achieve that, the better)?

All signs point towards Stig and Hans experiencing something extremely unusual in the woods that night. Whether they were attacked by alien jelly blobs or whether it was something else that the men simply could not comprehend, something happened. Something that we will likely never fully understand.

We can only hope that if the alien jelly creatures return for a second attack on Earth, that we have plenty of car horns and they haven't discovered ear plugs.

Interestingly, there is another even earlier report of a human encountering amoeba-like ETs. It occurred in Peru one night in 1947, when a witness spotted a metallic disk parked next to the highway outside of the city of Lima. He made his way over to the disk, curious as to what it was. When he got close to the saucer, he was greeted by two creatures that looked like oversized single cell organisms. Each was between five and six feet tall, their skin was the colour of sand and coarse in texture, and they looked like bananas that were joined together.

These jelly bags were far friendlier than the ones Hans and Stig would meet just over a decade later, and they spoke to the witness. Or rather, they communicated with him *somehow*. The creatures lacked mouths, but the witness heard words in English (strange that they didn't communicate in Spanish, but luckily the witness knew English) that he said sounded like they came from a speaker. Whether this was a literal speaker or some form of telepathic communication is unknown.

They told him that their species did not reproduce in the same way that humans did, and demonstrated this by separating and splitting their beings into more versions of themselves, just like microscopic organisms on Earth. This method of reproduction may sound quite depressing, but these jelly bags still get more action than most of the ufologists who research them.

With this demonstration over, the voice asked if the witness would like a tour of their craft. Who could say no? The man entered the disk and was…pretty underwhelmed. He described the inside of the UFO to be quite dull and empty. Perhaps sensing their new human friends' disappointment with their spaceship interior and feeling slightly embarrassed, they cut the tour short. They ushered him back outside, and quickly took off. This witness would not talk about his encounter for twenty years, and even when he did, he insisted on remaining anonymous.

Could these amoeba aliens have been the same that Hans and Stig met in the woods that night? Could the aliens that the Swedish pair met have been dragging them towards their UFO, not to abduct or harm them, but to show off how much nicer the inside was now? Had they gone back to their home planet, humiliated by the reaction of the first human being to see the inside of one of their crafts, and had the whole thing refurbished? Was their ride now well and truly pimped?

If Hans and Stig had made it to the UFO, who knows what wonders they would have seen inside!

ABDUCTED BY INTERGALACTIC ROBOTS

Y ou can't talk about aliens without talking about alien abduction. Thanks to alien abductions in pop culture, we're all fairly familiar with how it works. Someone is minding their own business when all of a sudden they are scooped up by a brightly lit disc-shaped UFO. Once on board, they are met with a varied mix of short and tall grey humanoid creatures with large black eyes. They are then placed on a table and subjected to medical tests and experiments. Once the aliens have the data or specimens they need from their human guest, the person is returned to where he or she was found. After being dropped off, often the person will have a large gap of time missing from their memory. Sometimes the memory of the abduction will come to the surface on its own, other times it takes hypnotic regression therapy to find out what happened during the lost time.

The idea of being kidnapped and involuntarily experimented on by a race from beyond the stars is terrifying enough on its own. Sometimes though, even this experience is too ordinary. Some people have been unlucky enough to experience an alien abduction that makes the classic case seem like a welcome alternative.

On the evening of October 11, 1973, coworkers Charles Hickson and Calvin Parker headed out together. Charles was forty-two and Calvin was nineteen, and what they lacked in an age-appropriate friendship they made up for in a mutual love of fishing, and fishing was what was on the agenda that night. The location was the Pascagoula River in southeast Mississippi. Initially they had little luck, and decided to return to a spot that had yielded some fishy results for Calvin recently. They headed to a disused shipyard along the river and cast out from an old pier.

All was going well until around 9.00 PM when the men saw something strange. On the water, they saw the reflection of a blue light. Calvin panicked slightly, thinking that the light must have come from a police car that was there to move them on, but the men quickly realised that the light was not coming from a car on the bank… it was coming from above the river.

The men looked up and saw a blue light that seemed to pulse rhythmically. They guessed that it must have been about two miles away, and they were curious about what it could be. It was too near to be any sort of star or planet in the darkening sky, and it didn't look or behave like any aircraft the men knew of. "It's probably some natural phenomena, like swamp gas," the men thought. They continued fishing as the blue light looked down on them, but whatever was in the sky was about to take a much more active role in their night.

Soon Charles and Calvin realised that the blue light was getting closer. In fact, it looked like it was coming in for a lading. It descended with a zipping sound and hovered several feet above the ground about 100 yards away from the fishing men. It was now that the men realised that the blue light was emanating from a solid object, some sort of craft. Charles and Calvin were starting to realise that this blue object was certainly something more than a simple case of gas, swamp or otherwise. They described the craft as being in the shape of an egg on its side, with a small dome on top of it. Though it was close to the men and the night was silent, they could hear no noise coming from it. The men considered reeling in their lines and getting out of there, but it was already too late.

The men suddenly heard a buzzing sound coming from the object. Then a hatch or doorway opened on the side of the blue egg-shaped craft. Out of this hatch stepped three creatures. You would assume that after exiting the levitating craft, these creatures would have fallen unceremoniously to the ground, landing in an embarrassing pile. But they didn't. They floated in the air. And they were quickly floating towards the fishing men.

Charles and Calvin described the three creatures that stepped out of the blue UFO and floated towards them as being humanoids around five feet tall. They had wrinkly grey skin which was similar to an elephants. They had thimble-shaped heads that attached to their shoulders without a neck. Their mouths were just slits, they had no eyes, and where their ears and nose should have been were thin pointy conical protrusions. They had long arms that ended in claws or pincers. They had stumpy legs that seemed almost fused together, which looked like an elephant's foot. The description of the creature's feet and skin would earn them the moniker of the Pascagoula Elephant Men.

As the creatures approached the men, Charles and Calvin realised that they moved in an odd way; they seemed almost mechanical. When one of the creatures attempted to communicate with electronic sounding buzzing noises, they started to think that maybe these things weren't creatures at all...maybe they were robots!

The men, unable to understand or respond to their robotic buzzing language, just remained still. They were too shocked to do anything. Suddenly, two of the three robo-creatures grabbed Charles with their crustacean-like claws and lifted him into the air as if he were weightless. The third scooped Calvin up, who passed out instantly. Whether this was out of fear or whether one of the elephant men injected him with a sedative is unknown. They glided back towards their waiting ship with the two men.

Charles and Calvin were brought onboard the oblong UFO and were blinded by the bright light inside. The men were quickly separated. Charles was left physically paralysed and floating in a white room. He could only move his eyes, and he looked around to see what else was in the area. There seemed to be nothing else in there with him. That was until something emerged from the wall. A robotic eye the size of a basketball was now scanning Charles all over. It went around his back, down to his feet, then came face to eye with him. Charles noted that the electric eye was full of small mechanisms and gizmos, suggesting technology that was far more advanced than what was available to humans in 1973.

Charles felt the sensation of being grabbed by claws again, and before he knew it he was being dragged back out of the craft and was gliding over the ground next to the Pascagoula River. The elephant men dumped himself and Calvin back where they had found them, and the men watched as the blue-FO took to the skies. As the ship disappeared into the night sky, a strange message entered Charles' mind. It said "We are peaceful; we meant you no harm." Did he just receive a telepathic apology from the space-bots?

Calvin stared out over the water and asked Charles what had just happened. Calvin had no memory of what had happened to himself on the ship, but he could remember being flown to a UFO by robotic elephant men with pincers. The men headed back to Charles' car, where they sat for close to an hour and tried to comprehend what had just happened to them. The only conclusion they came to was that no one would believe them. Initially they decided to keep the whole thing to themselves, before realising they had to report it on the basis of national (or even international and worldwide) security. The men feared that their abduction was a precursor to a full on alien invasion.

Charles phoned a local air force base. He spoke to the base's sergeant who informed him that the military was no longer looking into UFO reports. At this point the idea of flying saucers and little green men had become all but discredited, and most people had lost interest in the possibility that we were receiving visitors from other worlds. Sure, maybe the US government was still investigating the phenomenon in secret, but in the public eye they wouldn't give it the time of day. The sergeant told Charles to tell his story to the local sheriff, believing a case of alien abduction was more suited to a small and rural police force.

Charles and Calvin were reluctant to speak to the law for two reasons. One, they thought there was no way they would be believed, and two, they weren't really meant to have been in the location that they were fishing (hence Calvin's fear of a police car earlier). Still, they decided that reporting the encounter was their patriotic duty. At the very least, they thought, they could prove that they weren't doing anything *too* illegal at the old shipyard. They could bring along a fish they had caught, which would prove they weren't brewing illicit moonshine or dumping a body out there.

The men went to the sheriff, and, to his credit, he listened to the story that Charles and Calvin had to tell. What's more, he believed them. Or, at least, he believed that something had happened by the river. He could see the men were badly shaken up, but he wasn't yet convinced that they were taken aboard an oddly-shaped blue UFO by wrinkly robots with pincers then examined by a mechanical eye while suspended in zero gravity. Sceptics, huh?

The sheriff was so doubtful of the men's story that he attempted the law enforcement's go-to trick when dealing with UFO witnesses. The sheriff thought that if the men were making up their story they wouldn't admit it to him, but they might discuss it in private.

After some probing (if you'll pardon the expression) the sheriff excused himself from the room, but left a hidden tape recorder running. He hoped to catch the men, not expecting to be spied on, discussing their fabricated story. The sheriff came back to the room sometime later and dismissed Charles and Calvin, telling them he'd contact them in the near future. When the abductees had left the police station, the sheriff listened to the tape and was surprised to hear men discussing their ordeal privately. Not only did the sheriff not find any evidence of the men lying, he thought they sounded more distressed when talking about it with him out of the room.

Charles and Calvin, despite their terrifying experience, went back to work the next morning. You can take days off for illness and bereavement, but sadly not alien abduction. The men tried to have as normal of a day as possible, while not mentioning what happened to them the previous night to anyone. A few hours into the workday, the men were told by their manager that they had a phone call. Confused, they walked to the office, scooped up the phone, and said "Hello?" On the other end was a reporter who wanted more information about the abduction. Charles told him he had no comment and hung up. How did this guy know about what had happened to them? They had only told one person about it. Charles phoned the local sheriff who told him that his office was also flooded with reporters.

The sheriff had, for some reason, leaked the men's story to the local press. Why he did this is unclear, but it's possible that he was asking the local newspaper if anyone had reported seeing anything weird the night before. It's equally possible that he was just a huge gossip. The men were shocked and angry; they wanted to keep their experience secret and felt that the sheriff had betrayed them by mentioning it to reporters. The men tried to lay low and avoid journalists, but it wasn't long before their leaked story spread from local news, to statewide, to countrywide, to worldwide.

Charles and Calvin did their best to avoid snooping reporters and tried to just let the whole thing blow over. When it became clear that things weren't just going to settle down and go back to normal for them anytime soon, they decided to speak to someone. But they weren't just going to speak to some journalist who would print their story with an amusing headline. They were going to speak to someone that could help them.

The story of the Pascagoula Elephant Men had reached the ears of ufologist and future Spielberg consultant J. Allen Hynek. Hynek and an associate travelled to meet the men, and interviewed them at length. The two men were questioned while hooked up to a polygraph (also known as a lie detector) machine, and there was no sign that either man was not telling the truth.

Hypnotic regression therapy was even attempted on Charles to try and extract more information about the abduction from the man's subconscious. While under hypnosis he was able to recall more details from the night in question and gave a version of the story that backed up his friend's.

After interviewing and testing the men, along with reading the original police report and listening to the secret audio recording the sheriff took, Hynek concluded that Charles and Calvin were telling the truth. He believed that the men had experienced, and were traumatised by, something "not terrestrial", which suggests that Hynek thought that the men saw something other than terrestrial. Possibly more than terrestrial. Perhaps even…extra-terrestrial? He concluded that no person could believe that the men were faking their experience after speaking to them. And if the man who invented the Close Encounter Scale says it, you can take it to the bank.

Interestingly, Charles and Calvin would end up at the very same air force base that was so uninterested in their encounter just days earlier. The men wound up at the base after becoming worried they had been exposed to dangerous radiation while onboard the UFO, and the air force were the only people with the equipment to check. While they were at the base, the military personnel suddenly seemed much more interested in the men's story than they were when Charles called them. They were interviewed at length and a sketch of one of the Elephant Men creatures was even made by a resident artist.

In the years following their experience on the Pascagoula River, Charles and Calvin tried to escape their unwanted UFO-related fame. It seemed that there was no escape, though; this story had captured the public's imagination and they wanted more and more information from the men. Eventually, Charles and Calvin reluctantly began to embrace their place as celebrities of ufology and began giving interviews and even writing their own books about the encounter.

What really happened to Charles Hickson and Calvin Parker on the bank of the Pascagoula River that night in 1973? Were they really abducted by mechanical elephant men and examined by a large robotic eye? It seems simply too bizarre to make up.

And if they did make it up, why? They were reluctant to call the air base and go to the police station. It was the local sheriff who leaked their story to the press, against the men's wishes. When reporters came sniffing around, the men avoided them as best they could. If making money was their goal, they were going a strange way about it. By the time they started to accept their place in the annals of ufology, years had already passed. Surely they made some money from book sales and interviews, but this seems to be more of a "If we're going to be questioned about this to the end of our days, we might as well get paid for it" attitude, rather than something that was planned. Apparently even million dollar Hollywood movie deals were offered at one point by producers and directors who wanted to tell the story on the big screen, but the men declined.

The story of the Pascagoula Abduction has lived on as one of the most famous cases of alien abduction ever reported simply due to how strange the whole thing was. From the unusual description of the UFO, to the wrinkly and pointy floating abductors, to the scanning eye device, it all just sounds too bizarre to have been made up by two entirely ordinary men with seemingly no ulterior motives of money or fame. The high strangeness in the Pascagoula case makes other famous stories of alien abduction, like the Betty & Barney Hill, Whitley Strieber, and Travis Walton cases, look entirely normal and usual by comparison.

Whether or not Charles and Calvin were abducted by flying mechno-elephant-men from another planet is always going to be up for debate, but in my personal opinion; Hynek believed them, and you don't argue with J. Allen Hynek.

GEF: THE TALKING MONGOOSE

Talking animals are usually reserved for animated movies and their poor quality live action remakes, but for a family on the Isle of Man in the 1930s, a talking animal became a strange reality. But this talking animal was no mere parrot imitating the vocal sounds made by humans. This wasn't even an animal that should be on the island. This talking animal was a small furry mammal known as a mongoose. And this mongoose was called Gef.

The Irving family lived on the Isle of Man, a small island in the Irish Sea, in a modest sized and isolated farmhouse. The family consisted of father James, mother Margaret, and daughter Voirrey. The Irvings lived a very quiet and simple life until one day in September 1931 when that quiet was broken by a scratching and clawing sound coming from inside their walls. They thought that surely a rat had just gotten in there somehow and soon left out traps to catch the sneaky rodent. The traps stayed empty, and the noises continued.

As the days went on, the sounds started to annoy and frustrate the family. James in particular was growing tired of the nuisance noises and decided to try a new tactic to get rid of the animal. He decided he was going to scare the creature so badly that it would flee the farmhouse altogether. He crept up to the wall, listened closely to where the sound was coming from, zeroed in on the animals location, and let out a growl. He attempted to make this noise sound as much like it was coming from some sort of large predator as possible, thus terrifying the smaller animal into leaving and never coming back. James was quite shocked when, instead of hearing the sound of small feet running for their life, the animal in the wall growled back at him.

The creature continued to live in their walls, and the noises it made started to get weirder. At points the family thought the creature even sounded human, and described noises it made as being similar to a baby. Like it was trying to talk, but couldn't quite manage yet. Having previously copied James' terrifying growl, the thing in the wall continued to show off its imitation skills. James would make various animal noises, such as bird calls, and the creature would repeat them. Even more impressive, the creature was able to remember these sounds. Before long, James could just say the name of an animal, and an impression of that animal would come from inside the walls. But animal impressions were just the beginning.

Thirteen-year-old Voirrey decided to teach whatever was in the walls something too. She began to recite nursery rhymes and asked the creature to repeat them back. Much to the shock of her mother and father, it did. It repeated the rhymes back clearly in a high-pitched voice. Before too long, the creature had evolved past the point of mere imitation. It seemed to have somehow learnt the English language.

One day the creature in the walls introduced itself to the Irving family. It told them that it's name was Gef, and that he was an extra clever mongoose. He went on to let them know a little bit about himself. He informed them that he was born in India in 1852. With this introduction, the family began an unusual relationship with the talking mongoose.

Things began happily enough and Gef even became like a fourth member of the Irving family. He moved out of the walls and into an alcove in the roof above Voirrey's bedroom. This little area they dubbed "Gef's Sanctum". During the days Gef would leave the farmhouse and wander the island. He'd pick up information here and there by listening in to conversations and reading the local newspaper. At night, he'd return back to the Irvings and tell them all that he'd learnt on his day's journey.

During this time when Gef first joined the family, no one had really *seen* him. He'd make noise, talk to the family, and even leave Margaret rabbits that he'd caught, but catching a glimpse of Gef proved difficult. It seemed almost as if he didn't want to be seen. James and Margaret caught quick glances of him on occasion, but it was Voirrey who he seemed to be most comfortable being seen by. She would describe Gef as being around the size of a rat, covered in yellow fur, with a long bushy tail that had black speckles on it. From this description, it would seem that Gef's claims of being a mongoose were true. Although, it would be later claimed that Gef also had tiny human hands; something that regular mongooses *do not* have.

You would assume that living with a gossipy talking animal would be all fun and games, but Gef was not the perfect houseguest. For a start, Gef gave the Irvings very little privacy. According to James, if you attempted to whisper anything, Gef would loudly announce that he knew what you were saying, then would repeat what you had just whispered. There were no more secrets when Gef was around.

He also had a temper. One morning when James was opening the mail, Gef must have thought he was taking his sweet time about it. He yelled out, "Read it out, you fat-headed gnome!" Another day while Margaret made her way towards the house, she began getting pelted with stones. She knew exactly who was behind this attack and shouted out to Gef, who called her a witch. Some days it seemed like Gef's entire goal was to torment and annoy the family. When asked why he was behaving this way, he'd tell them that he was doing it "for the devilment!"

Before long, the Irvings' neighbours became aware of Gef. Shockingly, some of them didn't instantly believe that the Irvings had a talking exotic animal living in their walls and wanted proof. A trip to the Irving farmhouse soon convinced them that the family was not lying. They would talk to Gef, and he would talk back. Some were even lucky enough to catch a quick glimpse of him. Eventually word of Gef reached the local newspaper and then reporters in England.

Newspapers in the UK dubbed Gef the "Dalby Spook" (named for the area on the Isle of Man where the farmhouse was located) and ran articles that didn't take the situation in the Irving home too seriously. These articles did catch the attention of Richard S. Lambert, editor of *The Listener* magazine, though. Richard decided to travel to the Isle of Man with the paranormal investigator Harry Price (who would later go on to investigate Borley Rectory, "The Most Haunted House in England!") to find out exactly what was going on at the Irving farmhouse. Gef, usually friendly enough to visitors, was not pleased when he was told that Harry Price was coming to the house. Gef reportedly said of Harry, "He's the man who puts the kybosh on the spirits!" Gef seemed worried that Harry was coming to disprove his existence.

As if in protest, when Richard and Harry arrived, Gef stayed hidden. Uncharacteristically, Gef even refused to talk or make any sound whatsoever. The Irving family were sure that Gef was still around somewhere, and they tried to coax some sort of sound out of him, but he would give them nothing. Harry then tried to appeal to the mongoose, telling Gef that they had come a long way just to meet him. Still, Gef stayed silent.

Richard and Harry left the island without proof. As soon as they were gone, Gef reappeared. Gef told James that he had gone on a short holiday while the visitors were in the area. He told him that he didn't want to meet Harry because he was a sceptic. James did manage to talk Gef into making some plastic casts of his teeth and claws and leaving a lock of his hair.

James sent these items to Richard and Harry and they quickly went about getting them tested. The casts of teeth and claws could not be identified by the Natural History Museum. The expert that examined them concluded that they belonged to no animal that he knew of, but definitely did not belong to a mongoose. He did say these moulds were possibly manmade, created by carving into the plaster with a stick. The hair sample likely belonged to a dog. The main suspect was the Irving family sheepdog, Mona.

Richard and Harry would publish a book about Gef in 1936 titled *The Haunting of Cashen's Gap*. In this book they spoke about Gef, their investigation into him, and his residency in the Irving home. In the book they remain fairly neutral and never say whether they believe in the Gef phenomena or not. In private, though, it seemed that Harry considered the whole thing a hoax.

Price wasn't the only investigator who came to visit Gef. The amazingly named parapsychologist Nandor Fodor also came to see if he could conclude what Gef was. The mongoose judged Nandor to not be worth performing for, and stayed silent and hidden for the duration of his stay.

Nandor was not as dismissive of Gef's existence as Price, though. After speaking to the family and many other people who had seen or heard Gef, he was convinced by their stories. Nandor was of the opinion that Gef was in fact an actual real-life mongoose. A mongoose that had been accidentally possessed by a split-off part of Jim Irving's personality, created through the father's belief that he had failed in life and could not accept it (Nandor's harsh words, not mine!). Having possessed a mongoose, it was then drawn back to its accidental creator to live in his walls and be an occasional nuisance.

As believable as this explanation is, there is one hole in it: where would a part of Jim's personality have found a mongoose to possess? This was the Isle of Man, after all. As it turned out, there may actually have been a mongoose or two on the island!

Two decades before Gef appeared, a local farmer had bought and released several of the creatures to keep rats at bay. Cats must have been scarce on the Isle of Man at the time. Could one of these mongooses have survived for twenty years? Could it have been wandering around, a totally normal animal, until one day it was suddenly possessed by a psychic manifestation that had broken off of Jim Irving?

As the 1930s continued, Gef appeared less and less to the Irving family. As the decade ended, he had all but disappeared. In 1945, James Irving died, and Margaret and Voirrey moved out of the farmhouse and off of the island. Actor Leslie Graham bought the house soon after and claimed to have shot and killed Gef. The animal he showed in pictures did not match the descriptions of the talking mongoose though, and Voirrey later identified the animal pictured as "not Gef". Why he would *want* to shoot a beloved magical mongoose in the first place was anyone's guess, let alone why he'd be proud of it.

Gef never appeared to any future owners of the farmhouse, or to any other residents of the Isle of Man. Until her death in 2005, Voirrey remained insistant that Gef was real and was not a hoax. She seemed reluctant to discuss Gef (even blaming the mongoose for why she couldn't find a husband) after moving and never tried to make money off the story, but when asked she would still remain adamant that her family did play host to a strange and sometimes mischievous talking mongoose.

What was Gef? Was he a cryptid? A ghost? An actual mongoose that had somehow developed the ability to speak? And how did he come to stay in the Irvings' farmhouse?

Gef seemed to have the abilities and characteristics of both a living creature and something like a phantom. He had a physical presence in the sense that he could make noise, throw stones, and interact with the environment around him. However, he also had the ability to appear and disappear at will. He could be invisible. He could listen in to conversation in the house and elsewhere on the island without the participants ever knowing he was there. Because of these reasons and more some people believe that Gef was a poltergeist.

Some believe that poltergeists are caused by, or at least attracted to, teenagers who are going through some sort of emotional problems. Due to this, many investigators have pointed to Voirrey as the reason Gef appeared and took up residence in the Irving home. While Voirrey may have not had any obvious issues she was going through, she was a very isolated person. Outside of her parents, she didn't have a whole lot of company. Any friends her own age she did have she would not have seen often, due to the rural location of the farmhouse. Could a poltergeist have been attracted to Voirrey's loneliness? Possible, but poltergeists are usually more of a violent spirit. Gef never seemed like he wanted to scare or harm the family; he was just a bit annoying sometimes. He did once tell the family that he could kill them all, but wouldn't, but that seemed to be an isolated incident. Mostly he seemed happy enough just living with the Irvings and occasionally being a pain in the ass.

If Gef wasn't a poltergeist, could he have been some sort of other ghost? According to the mongoose himself: yes! Gef once said, "I am a ghost in the

101

form of a weasel." This seems to imply that Gef is a spirit, but has chosen to appear as a small mammal. Why would he do this? I suppose it's less terrifying than having a full human apparition hiding in the walls and sleeping in your teenage daughter's bedroom. On other occasions Gef claimed to be "an earthbound spirit" and not a spirit at all, arguing that he wouldn't be able to kill rabbits if he were a ghost. He sure was one confusing mongoose. And that might give us a hint as to what he really was.

The Isle of Man, and particularly the area the Irvings' farmhouse was on, was associated with the fae. Fairies, imps, elves, gnomes, and more come under this heading. What they all have in common is their mischievous and trickster nature. A nature that is shared by our talking mongoose. According to legend, fae creatures could bring humans good or bad luck when they interacted with them. To win the favour of the fae, humans would leave out offerings of small trinkets, food, and drink. And the Irving family certainly left Gef some offerings. When he moved into the alcove in Voirrey's bedroom, they would leave him food. Bacon and chocolate were particularly unusual favourites of his. Gef even told the family that if they were kind to him, he would bring them good luck.

Could some sort of fae creature have taken the form of a mongoose and moved in with the family? Could the family have kept it around by, without realising it, leaving offerings to the creature?

There are plenty of people who share Harry Price's private opinion that the whole thing was a hoax. Many believe that the initial noises made by Gef and his speaking voice that came later were made by Voirrey. Sceptics say that Voirrey may have been a natural and immensely talented ventriloquist, with not only the ability to change her voice entirely but also to throw it so it sounded like it was coming from a different location entirely. Is this a talent that Voirrey could have discovered in her isolation and attempted to use to give her parents some entertainment in their equally as dull lives? Was it all just one big joke that got seriously out of hand? Did James and Margaret find out it was a hoax, but just played along for attention and a break in their monotonous existence?

If ventriloquism is the culprit, what of those who claimed to have seen Gef? Gef, annoyingly, would only appear to those who believed in him. This is why he ignored Harry Price during his visit. Gef only appearing to believers is a very convenient excuse as to why no investigators could ever get any proof of his existence. Sceptics point towards this as being evidence of Gef being a hoax. Those who claim to have seen Gef have been accused of only seeing what they wanted to see. If someone went into the Irving house, already believing that a talking mongoose was living there, they could be so desperate to catch a glimpse of one that their minds could trick them into seeing just that. Could sightings of Gef have just been a type of mass hysteria?

The loneliness and isolation of the Irving family may be the true cause of the existence of Gef, but not in the form of a hoax. Could the family have been so bored that they simply willed the entertaining Gef into existence by accident, using their latent psychic energy? This may sound far-fetched, but the concept of a thoughtform energy ghost, or a tulpa, is not a new one. It's a part of the Buddhist religion, a common concept in the occult, and has even been investigated by scientists. A point of debate is if you can create a tulpa by accident. If you can, could the Irvings have simply willed a small, furry, talking animal into existence to give them some entertainment without even knowing they were doing it? As more and more people started coming to the farmhouse, could Gef have just faded back into nonexistence?

Whether you believe that Gef was some sort of fae trickster spirit, a secret ventriloquist's joke, or a tulpa, this mongoose has gone down in history as one of the strangest stories in modern times. For such a ridiculous story, the public really got invested in it. People travelled for days to visit the Irving farmhouse in the hopes of hearing or seeing the mongoose. But why did Gef capture the public imagination so? James Irving summed it up when he said "No one would invent such a bloody silly story." In other words, Gef was simply *Too Weird To Be Fake!*

THE VAMPIRIC VEGGIEMAN

When it comes to encounters with strange beings, just about all of them are flesh and blood creatures.

Even beings that seem part mechanical, like the Sandown Clown and the Flatwoods Monster, are widely considered to be some sort of biological creature underneath a robotic suit. Very occasionally, though, an entity turns up that breaks this rule. Sometimes a creature will appear that isn't flesh and blood, but root and stem. Sometimes a creature is more flora than fauna. The Veggieman is one of these creatures.

In the summer of 1968, Jennings Frederick was in the woods near his father's property in Fairmount, West Virginia. He was out in these woods hunting woodchucks with a bow and arrow like a totally normal human being, but he was blissfully unaware that he was soon to become prey himself.

It was due to get dark soon, so he decided to head back to his dad's house. As he made his way home, he briefly stopped and rested against a tree. This was when he started to hear a strange sound. He described the sound as being similar to a record being played too fast. What made this sound stranger was that Jennings couldn't work out if he was hearing it from somewhere around him in the woods, or if it was in his head in the form of a telepathic communication. Whether the sound was exterior or interior, he listened closely to it and tried to work out exactly what it was.

As he concentrated on the sound, he soon began to make out words. Before long, he could hear the full message. It seemed to be a greeting and a plea for help. It said "You need not fear me," "I wish to communicate," "I come as a friend," and "I wish for medical assistance."

Jennings was confused. Was someone else in the woods with him, and were they hurt? Had one of Jennings arrows, meant for a woodchuck, gone astray and hit a civilian just out for a nice walk? Jennings reached for a handkerchief to dab his sweaty brow. Despite being late in the day the summer heat still beat down on him, and now he was also slightly nervous he had shot someone. Before he could reach his pocket, though, he felt a sharp pain in his hand which quickly spread up his arm. He thought he must have accidentally caught his hand on some sort of thorny plant. He looked down and was shocked to see that a thorny plant had caught *him*.

What gripped him was a hand that looked somewhere between human and vegetable. It was green, and it had only three fingers. Even stranger, each finger was seven inches long. The fingers ended in what looked like suction cups, and each cup had a needled spike inside of it. These suction cups had stuck to Jennings hand, and the needles had entered his flesh. He looked up from the green hand attached to his, following the creature's impossibly thin arm. This is when he saw the full body of what had grabbed him. It was over seven feet tall and humanoid. Its body was oddly shaped and looked like a plant stalk. Its arms were no thicker than the width of a coin. Its face was humanlike with large ears and yellow eyes, and the whole creature was a bright green in colour. It appeared to be a bizarre cross between man and plant.

Jennings stood frozen in this creature's grip. This was when he heard a sucking sound. Jennings once again looked to his hand, and he realised that the needle-like fingers that had pierced into his flesh were draining his blood. Pain ran up his arm again. He looked back to the creature's oddly human face, prepared to fight or scream, but he was stopped before he could.

As he looked at the plantman, its yellow eyes stared into him and started to change. Suddenly red appeared in the yellow, and it began to swirl. The red and yellow created a spiral that met in the middle to form orange circles in the centre of the creature's eyes. As Jennings stared into these eyes, he relaxed and the feeling of pain melted away. The creature was using this strange eye ability to hypnotise Jennings while it drained his blood like an oversized tick.

As Jennings fell under the plantman's mesmerism, it repeated its high pitched message of friendship and request for medical assistance. It was then that Jennings realised that when the creature appeared it looked sick and weak. As it drained more and more of his blood, though, it was looking healthier and healthier, like it had been given *Miracle-Gro*.

The draining process lasted mere minutes, though for a hypnotised Frederick it felt like a lifetime. When the creature had sucked all the blood it needed and looked in better shape, it loosened its grip and retracted its needle fingers from Jennings' flesh. It released him, and broke its hypnotic embrace. Before Jennings had a chance to react, the plantman took off running. It ran to a nearby hill at speeds Jennings thought impossible, then bound up it in leaps that were at least twenty-five feet in length. Soon it had crested the hill and disappeared behind it. Whatever was in Jennings' blood had truly revitalised the plantman, and then some!

As the creature disappeared, the pain in Jennings' arm suddenly returned. Then he heard a humming sound coming from the hill the creature vanished behind. Jennings was sure this sound came from a UFO the plantman had either taken off in, or from a UFO that had come to pick him up. No craft could be seen though, suggesting a high tech cloaking ability.

Jennings waited a moment until the sound faded away. He was unsure what to do next. Eventually he decided to head home, his plan before he had his weird encounter. Soon he arrived back at his father's house. He washed the puncture marks where the needles had stabbed into his flesh and bandaged his hand. He considered telling his father about his experience that day, but decided against it. In fact, he decided not to tell anyone about his bizarre encounter because he thought no one would ever believe it.

Jennings Frederick would develop an interest in the unknown after this encounter, and it was this interest that would eventually put him in touch with ufologist Gray Barker (former IFSB member, along with Albert Bender). Barker would finally share Jennings' encounter in the March 1976 issue of his newsletter, and the world would be introduced to the Veggieman (or the Vegetable Man, if you're addressing him formally).

Initially, it seemed as if Jennings was randomly accosted by a sick plant-like alien that needed some of his blood to get back to better health before flying his UFO home, but the meeting may have been more planned than initially thought. Meetings with weird entities seem to run in the family for many, and the Frederick family is no different.

Reportedly, Jennings' mother, one day years prior to her son's meeting with the Veggieman, while home alone and washing dishes in the kitchen, saw what she assumed to be a child on their property. She was worried this child might touch a nearby electric fence, so she ran out to warn the kid to stay away from it. When she got out of the house, though, she realised it was no child on the property.

What she saw was a short dark green creature that looked like a devil. It had pointy ears, a tail, and as far as she could tell, no face. The creature either didn't notice her, or just paid no attention to her. It was grabbing handfuls of

108

dirt and putting it in a container it was holding. As she watched this strange little figure at work, she noticed it had a wire or tube connected to it. The wire ran into some nearby grass and connected to a silver craft about five feet high and ten feet in diameter. The saucer sat on some sort of landing platform which had descended from its bottom, which gave the whole structure the appearance of a giant metal mushroom. The craft, or part of it, rotated while making a soft humming sound.

Mrs Frederick was terrified by this little devil man and ran back into the house, into the bedroom, and hid under the sheets. After some time she built up the courage to emerge from the covers and go back to the kitchen. From the window she saw the silver craft airbourne and flying away, now emitting a louder humming sound.

Jennings and his mother's story have some interesting similarities. First of all, both entities encountered are green. Both were described as having large ears. Both left in a craft that made a similar sound (though in Jennings' case, the craft was invisible). The main difference is the creature encountered by the mother was the size of a child, and the one encountered by Jennings was upwards of seven feet tall.

While the creatures were definitely not the same entity, could they be the same species? Perhaps both from different points in the life cycle of this alien race? Maybe they start out as small faceless devil-looking ETs before growing into massive and skinny plant-like beings (or vice versa!). The smaller being seemed to be taking samples from the Frederick property. Was this also what the larger being was doing, before falling ill and needing to drain Jennings' delicious and nutritious blood?

Jennings Frederick was under the instant impression that the Veggieman was some sort of extraterrestrial. With its strange appearance, abilities, and (possibly) leaving in an invisible UFO, it's easy to see why he jumped to this conclusion, but is it the case?

Could the Veggieman simply be an animal? Cryptids are thought to be creatures just undiscovered by science for the time being; could the Veggieman be a cryptid much like Bigfoot? There are even carnivorous species of plants in nature, like the venus fly trap. Could the Veggieman be some sort of evolution or mutation of a carnivorous plant? An evolution that bridged the gap between creature and flower? The ability to run, jump, and drink blood would certainly be an evolutionary leap. Not to mention the ability to communicate telepathically and use hypnotism!

Could Veggieman indeed be a plant, but of an unknown kind? In the world of the weirder than weird, there are other reported plants that have attacked humans. In 1874, German explorer Karl Liche described watching a tribe in Madagascar sacrificing one of their own to a tentacled tree. Though the Madagascar Tree is now thought to have been a hoax, there is another and more believed account of a plant attack.

In 1892, a naturalist known as Mr Dunstan reported his own encounter with a blood drinking plant in Nicaragua. He was out on work when he heard a pained noise from his dog. When he located the poor pooch, it was wrapped in what looked like a mesh of dark roots. He managed to cut his dog free using his trusty knife, but not without the plant putting up a fight. With his dog freed, he realised the canine had many small puncture wounds where it looked like blood had been drained. A blood draining mass of vines certainly sounds similar to our vegetable friend. Could the Veggieman be an evolution of this carnivorous cryptozoological plant?

Could the Veggieman have come not from another planet, but from another dimension? Could the multidimensional journey have sapped its energy and forced it to feed on Jennings for sustenance? Was the humming sound not evidence of an invisible UFO taking off, but the sound of a dimensional portal opening and closing as the Veggieman returned home?

Could the Veggieman have been an escaped scientific experiment? Could he have been quite literally grown in a lab by a government agency or mad scientist?

A final, and somewhat more radical, theory is that the Veggieman was a vampire. It needed to drain blood to survive, it had the ability to hypnotise and mesmerise its victim, it could run and jump great lengths at impossible speed; all traits found in vampire lore. Is it possible that a race of Veggiemen (or Veggiepeople) were once more abundant, and were the basis for the vampire legend? Could the legend have been adapted, and the creatures given a more human appearance, as the centuries passed? Could the blood draining thorny fingers have been replaced in the legend with fanged teeth? Could the basis for the entire vampire legend have started with blood-quaffing interdimensional plant men visiting from another plane of reality?

Perhaps in an alternate universe these changes to the lore were never made, and Christopher Lee appeared in *Dracula* movies painted green.

RUMBLE IN BOLIVIA: THE SHEPHERDESS VERSUS THE SHEEP SLAYER

The Chupacabra is one of the most well known cryptids in the world. Although its description changes slightly from encounter to encounter — sometimes it's more reptilian and sometimes it's more canine — the thing that remains constant is the creature's appetite. The Chupacabra has an insatiable thirst for the blood of livestock. Even the name *Chupacabra* literally translates into English as "Goat-Sucker".

This famous cryptid isn't the only bizarre entity on record with a taste for farmyard animals, though; extraterrestrials also seem to have an odd interest in our cattle. Farmers have been shocked to find cows, sheep, and goats killed overnight, drained of blood and harvested of organs. The wounds left on these creatures suggest a medical precision and technology in advance of our own. It seems that many of these mutilated cattle have had very technical surgery performed on them. But why? What would aliens want with animal blood and organs? Is it for research? Experimentation? Are ETs trying to reverse bio-engineer cattle for their home planet? No one knows. No one ever even really sees the aliens doing their impromptu veterinary surgery.

The only thing that really connects these dead animals to aliens, outside of the seemingly space age technology, is that strange lights are seen in the sky before the animals are found. Actual sightings of aliens hard at work on our Earth animals are rare, but the best and most detailed description may come from a fairly unlikely source: a Bolivian shepherdess.

In the southwestern highlands of Bolivia, Valentina and Gumersindo Flores lived and worked as farmers. One evening in 1967, Valentina led her flock of sheep and llamas into a new field to graze. Gumersindo was working elsewhere, but Valentina wasn't exactly alone; she was carrying their baby on her back like Luke Skywalker did with Yoda in *The Empire Strikes Back*.

When she got to this field, though, she noticed that only the sheep had made it. The llamas had broken off and wandered away at some point during their travels, as llamas are wont to do. Annoyed, Valentina rounded up sixty-four sheep in the grazing field and set off to find her wayward llamas.

Valentina found her llamas hanging out in a field almost an hour away from her sheep. You can't stay mad at a llama though, let alone a whole herd of them, so she cheerfully rounded them up and started the long trek back to her sheep and the grazing field.

When she, the baby, and the llamas arrived back in the field, though, she was annoyed to see that the sheep were not there! Things were starting to feel like a lazily written sit-com. Luckily, sixty-four sheep left a trail, and Valentina knew how to track her animals. The sheep tracks led her up a nearby hill and headed towards an old corral: a short, stone-walled roofless structure used to pen animals. As she approached the corral, she started to realise something was wrong. For one, she couldn't hear the tell-tale baa-ing of her sheep. What's more, there was some sort of fabric that had made a makeshift roof over the old pen. It looked like a type of mesh tarp.

Valentina was sure her sheep were in there, and she approached the corral. She could see through the thin webby substance that coated the pen, and saw the ground inside carpeted with sixty-three dead sheep. In the middle, an inexplicable figure held the sixty-fourth.

The humanoid figure was the size of a child or a very short man, barely three feet tall. It was wearing a one-piece leotard uniform with brown boots. On its back was a bag held on by red straps that crossed in the middle of the being's chest. It was wearing a large helmet that had a small propeller on top of it, like the popular children's cap. Its face was visible, and it had milky white skin, blue eyes, and an extravagant red moustache. In its hand was what looked like a tube that ended in a hook, and it was attached to the little humanoid by a chain. It didn't take much imagination to work out what it was doing with this hooked device. Next to it was a bag filled with sheep organs.

At this point, many people would have turned and ran, but Valentina was no shrinking violet. She didn't get scared, she got angry. In her native Bolivian tongue she called the little being every insult under the sun. When this didn't calm her down enough, she started throwing rocks at it. When a rock smacked its helmet, it was suddenly aware of Valentina's presence. It dropped the final sheep and jumped over to a metallic box that looked similar to a radio. It pulled a lever and the mesh substance that roofed the corral was sucked into the box.

At this point Valentina noticed an almost identical being outside the corral. This one ran up a nearby hill and sat on a chair. Something not unlike helicopter blades emerged from the back of this seat, and the second being took off into the air, leaving his friend on the ground with Valentina. Maybe it knew what was coming next.

Hucking rocks and insults at the small being hadn't extinguished the rage in Valentina. It had killed her sheep, it had destroyed her livelihood, and she wanted to kick its ass (assuming this species had asses). The trash talk was over, it was time for the fight to begin. If there was a crowd, it would have been going wild.

The stone walls of the corral were the ropes, the sheep corpses were the mat, and Valentina stepped into the ring to fight in the wrestling event of the millennium: The Shepherdess versus The Sheep Slayer in a match to decide the Hardcore Champion of the Universe. No holds barred, no disqualifications, no count outs.

She drew a small but tough stick she used while herding from its holster and approached her opponent. The little being tried to speak to her, but it was in no language the Shepherdess knew. It tried to plead with her in Alienese, but it was no use. The smackdown was inevitable.

She swung her makeshift weapon at the moustachioed Sheep Slayer and cracked it over the head. It started to scream, and blood began to run down its face. The Sheep Slayer knew it had to defend itself. It sliced at the Shepherdess with its hook weapon. It cut into Valentina, but by sheer luck was stopped from seriously hurting her by the knot in the satchel she used to carry her baby (she was fighting an alien while still carrying her kid!). The hook device snapped back into the Sheep Slayer's hand by means of the chain it was attached to. The Sheep Slayer knew it had messed up. The Shepherdess charged again, swinging her club. It tried to block her blow, and while it may have prevented another hit to the head, the smack to the arm proved to be almost as bad. Something in the creature's limb snapped. Blood began to run out of the sleeve of the being's one-piece uniform.

The Sheep Slayer knew it had met its match. With his uninjured arm he grabbed his metallic box that the mesh fabric sucked back into and his bag of guts, then ran out of the corral and up to a seat just like the one his colleague had sat/flown in. The Sheep Slayer took off in the same helicopter-fashion and, quicker than a hiccup, it was gone.

With the match abandoned, the Shepherdess was victorious. Doubtless the Sheep Slayer knew he was mere seconds away from being smacked with a folding chair, chokeslammed through a table, and being pinned for a three-count.

Valentina scooped up her one remaining living sheep and left the ring. Though she had won the match, the belt, and the title, she didn't feel like much of a champion. The hellacious hirsute heel had hurt her in a non-physical way. With a large portion of the livestock now dead, Valentina knew that she and her family would have no choice but to leave their farm.

When she arrived home and told Gumersindo about her sci-fi slobberknocker, he reported it to the Bolivian government and they dispatched the army to investigate. They apparently took this matter so seriously that armed forces were on the scene in time to collect the sixty-three deceased sheep and some samples of the alien blood that Valentina had spilled in the ring. The sheep were found to be missing vital organs and most of their blood. As for the blood collected from the small being? No findings have ever been revealed.

What the little helmeted being with a red moustache and his flighty friend wanted with the insides of sixty-three sheep is unknown. Whether these creatures use them for research, experiments, or whether they just collect them like *Pokémon* cards is unclear. The fact is that reports continue to come in of cattle who have been killed and harvested of blood and organs by unknown perpetrators who seem to not be of this Earth. Whether they come from another planet, reality, or dimension is (as with everything else in this book) up for debate.

117

When J. Allen Hynek was coming up with his Close Encounter Scale, he didn't account for one thing: there's no Encounter Level for beating the crap out of an alien. Valentina Flores is not only one of the few people who can say they've caught an extraterrestrial mutilating livestock in the act, she's in the even more exclusive group of people who can say they've gone toe-to-toe with a creature from another planet and won.

If someday an alien invasion of Earth should happen, we won't need to call on the military. We won't even need Jeff Goldblum armed with a computer virus to fend them off. If we want to beat an extraterrestrial invasion, all we need is a couple of pissed off Bolivian shepherdesses.

THE MISSOURI ALIEN PENGUINS

V isitors from other worlds come in all shapes and sizes.

Usually they appear in a form that we can understand, whether it's the very human looking Venusian aliens that visited George Adamski in a California desert with a message of peace, or the still very humanoid greys that abducted Travis Walton and subjected him to medical tests and examinations.

Sometimes, though, they are beyond comprehension. In these cases, our feeble human brains try desperately to grasp some reference point to describe these indescribable creatures. For two kids on the Isle of Wight, it was a clown. For Hans and Stig outside of Domsten, it was amoebas. For the residents of a farmhouse in Hopkinsville, it was goblins.

For one man, the only thing he could equate the entities he was seeing to was penguins.

On February 14, 1967, sixty-four-year-old Claude Edwards was gearing up to celebrate Valentine's Day with a hard day of work on his farm in Tuscumbia, Missouri. He started off his day like he had hundreds of times before, by walking from his house to his barn. As he walked, he realised that something was different this morning, though. For a start, most of his cattle were huddled together. Stranger still, they were all facing the same direction, staring at something. Claude stopped in his stride, confused. He followed the eyeline of the cattle to see what they were all looking at. He quickly saw what had them acting so weird. Parked in the meadow next to his barn, he saw a flying saucer.

The craft was roughly eighteen feet wide, and coloured a metallic green. It had small circular windows through which coloured lights could be seen. It was held up by some sort of metal tube, which gave the whole thing the appearance of a giant mushroom (very similar to the description of the craft seen by Jennings Frederick's mother in the Veggieman case!).

Claude continued towards his barn, getting closer to the UFO with every step. He reached the barn and made sure it was locked (safety first). He then began walking towards the metal mushroom. He was roughly seventy feet away from the craft, separated from it by a couple of fences and some cows. With this closer look and better vantage point, he not only got a better look at this UFO parked on his property but also now noticed that several of its occupants were out in his field.

The beings that were now scampering around the flying saucer were like nothing Claude had ever seen before. They were like nothing *anyone* had ever seen before. Each one was around three feet tall. They were each wearing a one piece outfit that was a grey/green in colour; similar to their ship. They were wearing dark goggles with the eyes set far apart. They had a protrusion poking out from where their mouths should be that looked similar to a gas mask. Their arms were short and stumpy. They had no hands that Claude could see, their arms seemed to end with flippers. Their legs were either non-existant or obscured. It is unknown how the creatures physically looked as these shiny emerald suits covered their entire being. Despite their hidden legs, they moved around quickly and frantically. All this combined made Claude think of green penguins from beyond the stars.

Claude was alarmed, but he was a farmer and he couldn't have trespassers waltzing (or waddling) about, even if they were avian aliens. He picked up a couple of rocks from the ground with the intention of chucking them at the UFO and damaging it to the extent that it was unable to take off. With their craft out of commission, presumably the tiny trespassers would just have to sit and wait while Claude called the authorities to arrest them. What could go wrong?

Claude walked through his field, dodging around cows and jumping the fences, towards the craft and creatures. He was almost within throwing range, he just had to take a couple more steps. He got to within fifteen feet of the craft, and...smack.

Claude walked face first into a forcefield. Like a videogame character trying to go into an out-of-bounds area, he was stopped dead in his tracks by an invisible wall. He took a couple of steps back and threw one of his rocks. It bounced off the invisible barrier. As he threw a second rock with a similar result, the alien penguins began to rush back to the craft. The metal cylinder must have had some sort of entry hatch out of view, as the penguins went behind this tube and disappeared into the ship. Presumably the tube contained either an elevator or spiral staircase.

With all the little green creatures back inside the craft, the saucer began to move. It tilted back and forth a couple of times before it took off, levitating upwards. Once airborne, the craft took off at speed and left Claude's field of vision.

Claude's story was eventually told to UFO investigator Ted Phillips by Claude's brother. Ted was so struck by the bizarre nature of the story that he made his way to the farm in Tuscumbia to meet the man himself and inspect the area where the alien penguins and the metal mushroom were seen.

When Ted arrived at the farm and told Claude why he was there, he didn't receive the warm welcome he had perhaps been expecting. Claude told him that he wouldn't be saying a word unless one condition was agreed on: Ted would not reveal Claude's identity in regards to his encounter. Ted agreed, and held up his side of the bargain until Claude passed away.

With this agreement made, Ted was not shocked to find out what type of man Claude was. He was an honest man who before his encounter had not believed in one bit of this flying saucer nonsense, but Claude knew what he saw, and he wasn't going to back down on what he swore was the truth.

He told Ted the full story and then took him out to the meadow by the barn where the whole thing happened. Luckily, the forcefield seemed to have departed with the UFO, but evidence that something was there remained. Where the tube beneath the saucer, the mushroom stem, met the ground was an indent one metre in diameter. The earth inside this circle was dehydrated and nothing like the soil that surrounded it. Something had definitely sat here. Could it really have been an alien spacecraft full of little green penguin people?

The reason why the alien penguins visited Claude's farm in their mushroom ship is unknown, but knowing what we know about extraterrestrials and their interest in livestock, perhaps we can hazard a guess. Could these beings have landed on the farm with the intention of performing their usual unusual surgery on Claude's unsuspecting animals? Was Claude close to witnessing the phenomena known as Cattle Mutilation that we previously discussed in the story of the Sheep Slayer? The cows on the farm certainly seemed concerned by what they were seeing. Perhaps a fear of aliens is a part of the bovine collective unconscious.

As we know, very few people ever see this act actually happening. Usually it happens in the dead of night, and the only evidence of alien involvement is lights in the sky and the advanced surgical technology seen on the animals. Could the alien penguins have landed with the intention of performing secret surgery on the cattle, but failed to take into account that farmers get up extremely early? Were they taken by surprise when Claude turned up in the early AM and approached them, rocks in hand, and bumped into their ship's forcefield? Were they so taken aback by this that they had to waddle back into their ship and leave empty handed (empty flippered?)?

Claude Edwards never attempted to make any money off his story. He didn't even want his name associated with the story until after he was dead. All Claude had to gain by telling his story was disbelief and ridicule. But he told it anyway, because that's the kind of guy he was. He saw what he saw, and he wasn't going to lie about it.

As Claude did not share his story of green alien penguins invading his farm while he was alive, it's unknown how many people would have laughed at him. But laughing at a man who was fully prepared to smash a piece of advanced alien technology from outer space with a few rocks just for having the nerve to land on his property would maybe not have been the wisest idea.

INDRID COLD: THE GRINNING MAN

I s there anything creepier than a stranger smiling maniacally at you? Of course there is, but it's still pretty unsettling. The creep factor can be upped, though, when the person smiling at you seems to be from another world. If the person smiling begins to talk to you telepathically and looks like Iggy Pop from the *Lust For Life* record cover, the creep factor goes through the roof.

On the night of November 2, 1966, a sewing machine salesman named Woodrow Derenberger was driving to his home in West Virginia on Interstate 77 when he heard a crash. Woodrow looked back, worried that one of his sewing machines had fallen over. While he was looking back, he saw through his rear window what looked like a vehicle approaching. Woodrow was nervous, as he had been speeding slightly and thought it might be a police car getting ready to turn on the lights and pull him over. This vehicle suddenly overtook Woodrow at great speed and blocked the road in front of him, causing him to slam on the breaks. What had cut in front of Woodrow was no police car, it was some sort of flying craft.

He described this UFO as looking like an old fashioned kerosene lamp, coloured charcoal grey. A hatch opened on the side of the craft, and a tall man (or what looked like a man) emerged. Woodrow stayed in his car, so shocked by what he was seeing that he couldn't move, let alone drive. The man from the craft approached the car, and Woodrow saw that he was wearing a shimmering green suit with some sort of long jacket over the top of it. He had suave dark brown slicked back hair. As he got closer, Woodrow saw the man's huge grin.

The man walked up to the side of Woodrow's car and asked him to roll the window down. When he asked him this, the large smile didn't leave his face. In fact, his mouth didn't move at all. He had asked Woodrow to do this telepathically. Woodrow, either because he felt this man was no threat or due to some telepathic force, did as he was asked. Why the man wanted the window down is anyone's guess, as he still continued to communicate telepathically. Maybe it was just a matter of good manners.

The man told Woodrow that he meant him no harm, which was a relief. He asked Woodrow his name, and he answered; "Woody". The grinning man then introduced himself as Indrid Cold, which has the be the coolest name this side of the galaxy. He then asked Woodrow what the city lights in the distance were. Woodrow tried to explain the concept of a city to Cold, and he seemed to understand. He informed his new friend that where he was from, such places were called "Gatherings". The two spoke for several minutes, and Cold implied he was here to learn more about humanity, referring to himself as a "Searcher".

Cold told Woodrow to report their meeting and telepathic conversation to the authorities, and assured him that he would come forward at a later date to prove that Woodrow was telling the truth. Cold then told his new friend that he would see him again. Indrid Cold walked back to his grey lantern-shaped UFO, entered, and took off.

Woodrow drove home, and when he got there his wife could tell something was wrong with her husband. He told her the full story, and she told him he should go to the police. Woodrow decided this was a good idea, and besides, Indrid

Cold said that he should. The police seemed to take his story seriously, quite rare for a report of this sort in this time period.

The next day, Woodrow's story of meeting an alien entity called Indrid Cold on a nearby highway exploded in the local press. Woodrow even did a thirty-minute-long live television interview where he told his story and even took questions. He answered such important questions as "Were there windows on the UFO?", "Do you drink?", and "Why do you think he went to the left side of your truck, and not the right?"

In the wake of this interview, some people did come forward to back up Woodrow's story. He claims that while he was having his conversation with Cold, cars did occasionally pass, and they likely would have seen the two men and possibly even the UFO, which was hovering roughly fifty feet above the road as they spoke.

One person claimed that a man matching the description of Indrid Cold had tried to get his attention on the road that night, but he kept driving. Maybe this was when Indrid decided he needed to block the road with his craft if he was going to get a conversation out of anyone. A mother claimed she stopped her car on the highway when she saw the craft, and she and her two children watched the lamp-shaped UFO take off. Another man said that Indrid's craft had appeared above his car and flashed a bright light at him.

These people could all just be trying to get in on Woodrow's story, or they could be telling the truth. Either way, Woody quickly became a local celebrity. Rumours began to fly wild about Woody and his alien pal. Some people even believed that the extraterrestrial had gotten Woodrow knocked up, and he was now expected to birth a child that was half human and half alien. Obviously this was not true, mainly due to one glaring error that I'm sure you've already picked up on, but also because Indrid was a total gentleman and never put the moves on any of us Earthlings.

People started to flock to Woodrow's farmhouse every night, trying to see if Cold would return like he had promised. While all eyes were on the sky impatiently awaiting the descent of a UFO and the emergence of a smiling telepathic alien, an unassuming black car drove up to Woodrow's home almost entirely unnoticed by the crowd that surrounded it. A man in a black suit got out, knocked on the door, and he and Woodrow talked for a few minutes. Woodrow told his grinning friend that ever since their first meeting he had been experiencing a stomach illness. Indrid gave him a vial of some unknown substance that he assured Woodrow was medicine. He quaffed the potion, and instantly his symptoms cleared. The man in the black suit got back in his very ordinary car and drove through the crowd of sky watchers and off of Woodrow's property.

By March of 1967, the crowds who desperately wanted a glimpse of a UFO had lost interest and abandoned their nightly sky vigil on Woodrow's front lawn. With the coast now clear, Cold was able to abandon his very human vehicle and return to his spaceship. He would visit Woodrow multiple times by simply landing on Woody's farm and, if Woodrow hadn't noticed the intergalactic starcruiser on his property, he would send him a telepathic message asking him to come outside. Hopefully he was never in the bath at the time.

Woodrow would eventually be allowed inside Cold's craft, which he interestingly described the interior of as being pretty ordinary, and taken on journeys. In one instance, he was taken on a very local trip to Brazil. In another, Indrid took him a little further afield. He took Woodrow to his semi-nudist homeworld of Lanulos in the Ganymedes galaxy. Here, on this Earth-like planet, Woodrow met Indrid's family and learned about their people's culture, while the locals all ran around in nothing but colourful shorts.

When returned to his farmhouse, now full of strange encounters and alien knowledge, it's no surprise that Woodrow started work on a book called *Visitors From Lanulos*. In this book he intended to tell the world all about Indrid Cold and his people. But, as we know, there are certain people or entities out there who aren't fond of alien information being shared.

As Woodrow worked on his book, he began to receive anonymous phone calls that warned him to stop writing. When that didn't work, his wife began receiving similar calls. She was told to stop her husband, or *they* would. Indrid would write things down, only for the papers to mysteriously disappear. Occasionally he would come home and find his writing and notes riffled through and his tape recorder destroyed.

One day, while at work at an appliance store, Woodrow received a visit from the Men in Black. Two men in black suits entered the store, walked up to Woodrow, and told him to forget about everything he had seen. They left before Woodrow could react or respond.

The harassment of Woodrow and his family continued until his book was finally released in 1971. Visits from Cold continued even after that. Sometimes he'd arrive in his spaceship, sometimes he'd arrive by car. Sometimes he'd even bring friends and family with him. Sometimes he wouldn't even visit physically, he'd just chat with Woody telepathically. As for Indrid today? Some believe he perished in a spaceship crash, while others believe he still lives and even visits Woodrow's children.

Woodrow's meeting with Indrid was strange. But what was even stranger was that just weeks after their first meeting, the nearby town of Point Pleasant was assaulted by all manner of the paranormal. UFOs were seen, poltergeist activity was reported, the Men in Black stalked the streets, and Mothman took to the skies.

During this time period of high strangeness, Indrid may have appeared in a local house. A family in Point Pleasant was experiencing paranormal activity in their home. Activity was reported that would not be out of place in a classic haunting, but things jumped up a notch. In their daughter's room they reported seeing strange lights that would appear and move as if controlled by some intelligence. Things came to a head one night when the daughter woke up to see a tall man standing at the foot of her bed. A man that was smiling an impossibly wide smile.

The girl was shocked, but remained silent. This was until the man started to walk around the bed towards her. She covered her head with the blankets and screamed in terror. When her parents burst into the room, the man was gone. There was no sign of breaking and entering, and nothing was stolen. It was as if the man had just materialised in the girl's room then just as quickly disappeared. Was this unknown man actually Indrid Cold visiting another West Virginia resident? Or, if not Cold himself, was it another of his race?

This figure was described as wearing a chequered shirt, which is quite a bit more smart/casual than what Indrid was described wearing by Woodrow. Is it possible that there was more than one grinning man? Or Is it possible that Indrid just had several outfit changes? The change from catsuit to casual is almost reminiscent of David Bowie's persona change from the glam rock star of *Diamond Dogs* to the everyman soul singer look of *Young Americans*. Could Indrid Cold be considered an intergalactic Bowie?

Interestingly, a similar encounter happened in Scotland just a few years later in 1973. In the Crosshill area of Glasgow a woman was asleep next to her husband when she inexplicably awoke early in the morning. When she opened her eyes, she saw something unexpected illuminated by the moonlight. At the foot of the bed was a tall, bald man in some sort of leotard who was grinning maniacally.

130

He was moving strangely, almost robotically. The woman screamed, waking her husband who leapt out of bed and turned the light on. When the room suddenly brightened, it was just the man and his wife in it. Just like in Point Pleasant, nothing was stolen and there was no sign of breaking or entering. This Glasgow entity became known as the Gurning Man (gurning being the act of contorting one's face), very close to the Grinning Man, both in name and appearance.

This wasn't the first time the Gurning Man had been seen. Just days before his bedroom appearance, two teenage girls had seen him on a nearby street early in the morning as they walked home from a party. He stood under a streetlight, moving in an unusual, jittery manner. As the girls got closer, they noticed his weird appearance and the fact he was wearing some manner of catsuit. What scared the girls most of all though was his grin. The girls sped past this weird man and looked back. He seemed to have vanished into thin air.

A few days *after* the Gurning Man appeared in the couple's bedroom, a woman saw him in the street as she was putting milk bottles out. He was running in place and smiling at the woman. She stared at this strange sight, unsure of what to make of it. Suddenly the Gurning Man vanished into thin air right before her eyes.

This Scottish Indrid Cold was spotted multiple times over several months before he just vanished as suddenly as he had appeared. Could this have been Indrid himself, or another one of his kin? And what was his goal? Indrid seemed more friendly while his Scottish cousin gave the impression of simply wanting to creep out Crosshill locals.

Back in the States, two youths may have had an Indrid encounter that predates Woodrow's by mere weeks.

On the evening of October 16 in 1966, two boys were hanging out near their homes in New Jersey when they saw something weird. As they walked down a local street, they saw a man standing behind a fence just off the road. Even at a distance, they could tell something was off about this man, but they continued towards him. The man seemed to not notice the boys, and his attention was on a house across the street. As they got closer, they noticed that the man was tall, bald, and curiously wearing some sort of shimmering green one-piece suit.

As they got closer, they kept their eyes on the tall green man. When they were within arm's reach of him, he was suddenly aware of their presence. He slowly turned and looked at the boys, then flashed them an impossibly large smile. The boys were suddenly struck with an intense fear and took off running home. It was only later, after the boys had calmed down, that they started to recall more details about the man. They were caught off guard by his large and surreal smile and for a while that was all that remained in their minds, but soon they remembered things even weirder than an ear-to-ear grin. The man had small and beady eyes that were set unusually far apart, and he had no ears or nose.

Later that night, on that same street, rumours started to circulate that a woman had been chased by a tall man in green.

Theories on who or what Indrid Cold was are vast. Considering he appeared to Woodrow Derenberger in a UFO and claimed he came from another planet, calling him an alien is an easy conclusion to come to. Whether his meeting with Woodrow was pure chance or if he had been predetermined as Indrid's human contact is a point of debate.

Some have questioned why, if Indrid was an alien, did he look so human? The answer, to some, is simple: he was a shapeshifter. Indrid (and his friends

132

in New Jersey, Point Pleasant, and Glasgow, if they weren't all the same entity) took on the appearance of a human. Or at least attempted to. Forgetting to include ears and a nose in New Jersey may have been an oversight.

The smile, as unnerving as it was, may have been an attempt to appear less scary to us humans. Perhaps in their research they realised that smiling puts our species at ease and suggested friendship. Maybe Indrid and his co-workers back on Lanulos reasoned that the quickest and easiest way for Cold to make friends here on Earth was if he had a smile. And the bigger the smile, the more friendly the appearance. It is possible they did not consider that an inhumanly large smile from non-existent-ear-to-non-existent ear would have the opposite effect and scare the hell out of us and our poor unevolved human brains.

Some have pointed out that Indrid's meeting with Woodrow coinciding with UFO sightings, paranormal activity, Men in Black meetings, and the appearance of Mothman in the nearby Point Pleasant cannot be a simple coincidence. Could Indrid, UFOs, ghosts, the MIB, and even Mothman have all come from the same place? Some theorise that all aspects of the paranormal and supernatural are related, and all spawn from the same location. Could all of these beings have come from another dimension or layer of reality? Could the veil that separates our world from others be especially thin in places like Point Pleasant? Could the veil even have ripped, allowing all sorts of interdimensional beings to flood through and interact with, scare, and annoy people in our world?

Could other locations where Cold (or his Lanulos brethren) have been sighted have also had strange influxes of paranormal activity? Or, in these locations, was the tear between realities so small that only one weird thing could wiggle through at a time? Perhaps there was a scuffle at the other end of the dimensional tear and Glasgow was close to getting a Yeti stalking the streets before the Gurning Man muscled his way through.

And what is Indrid Cold's connection to the Men in Black? The MIB harassing Woodrow after he started to write his book is expected of them, but a deeper connection may be there. I'm sure it's not lost on anyone that Indrid once travelled to Woodrow's house in a black car wearing a black suit. Even his appearance isn't too unlike some Men in Black descriptions. Indrid was obviously much more friendly than his ufologist-scaring counterparts, and even encouraged Woodrow to report their meeting. Could the Lanulosians be the good counterparts to the evil MIB? If this is the case, then why were the grinners in New Jersey, Glasgow, and Point Pleasant so much more scary to those they appeared to than Indrid was to Woody?

Perhaps the main question Indrid left us with is: was there one grinning man or were there multiple grinning men? Was Indrid Cold the same entity that was spotted in New Jersey, Glasgow, and at the foot of the young girl's bed in Point Pleasant? Every one of these grinning men varied in appearance slightly, which suggests that maybe Indrid wasn't responsible for every single sighting of a tall smiling stranger. Were multiple beings from the planet of Lanulos visiting Earth and appearing to us humans? Or was Indrid just prone to shape-shifting and costume changes?

Of course, some say that Woodrow (and everyone else who met a grinning man) made up the entire encounter. Some say Woody fabricated the whole thing for fifteen minutes of fame and a quick paycheque. While this is of course a possibility, Woodrow never recanted or changed his story in all his years telling it, and he insisted it was the truth right up until his death in 1990.

While it's true he made some money from his books and appearances at UFO events in the years after his meeting with Indrid Cold, at the time it was very difficult for him. In the late 60s and early 70s, people who came forward to talk about UFO sightings and alien experiences were met with derision, ridicule, and mockery.

Woodrow's life was made much more difficult by talking about his meeting with Cold and continuing to do interviews and take questions on the subject. At points I have no doubt he wished he had just stayed quiet about the whole thing and stuck to selling sewing machines.

Maybe Woodrow's story would have been told and forgotten shortly after by most, remembered as just a footnote in the UFO world, but the fact that the same — or at least similar — beings were seen around the same time gave the story a lot of credibility. This, and the connection to Mothman and Point Pleasant, made the story believable to many. Not only was Woodrow's story thought to be too bizarre to have been made up, the fact that more and more people had their own strange stories that connected to it, made it one of the biggest stories in the history of ufology.

Whether Cold or another Lanulos resident will appear to a member of our race is unknown. But if you see a tall, bald figure in a shiny catsuit smiling impossibly wide at you as if they are on some sort of amphetamine, get ready for things to get weird because it might be something far stranger than a crazed glam rock star.

THE THREE-LEGGED ENFIELD MONSTER

At 9.00 PM on the 25 of April 1973 in Enfield, Illinois, ten-year-old Greg Garrett was attacked by a monster. He was playing in the backyard of his home when suddenly and without warning he was face-to-face with a nightmare. Whether this creature from beyond the young boy's imagination was actively trying to harm him or if Greg was just in its way is unknown. Either way, a brief melee ensued where the beast slashed at the boy with claws and snapped at him with fangs. Luckily, the boy was able to escape the monster's clutches before any serious injuries were sustained.

Greg ran inside and started to tell his parents what had happened just outside their home. Their child was badly shaken but managed to explain what he had just experienced. He told his mum and dad that he was attacked by a creature slightly taller than himself. It had talons, sharp teeth, and too many limbs. They thought that surely their son's imagination had just run away from him. But if he just imagined the whole thing, why were his clothes ripped?

While the Garretts were trying to work out what happened to their son, their neighbours Mr and Mrs McDaniel were returning home. They entered the house, and their kids ran up to them, scared out of their minds. "Dad, dad! Something's trying to break in!" they yelled. They told their parents that something had been trying to get into the house, clawing at the doors and windows, and it wasn't human. Mr McDaniel tried to calm the kids down, explaining it was probably just some animal.

That was when he heard a scratching at the door behind him. Expecting nothing more extraordinary than a stray dog looking for some scraps of food, he opened it. Standing at the front door of the McDaniel house was no dog. It wasn't even a kangaroo (McDaniel was very clear on this, he used to have a pet kangaroo so would know if it was). What stood at the door was a four- to five-foot-tall grey creature with a short stumpy body. It had two short arms that ended in clawed hands. It had two huge eyes the size of flashlights that glowed pink out of a head that seemed to have sunk into its body. It had a mouth full of jagged teeth. It was disgustingly described as both hairy *and* slimy at the same time. Perhaps strangest of all, the creature had three legs.

Henry McDaniel slammed the door shut, begrudgingly admitted that maybe his kids were right, and grabbed his gun. He threw the door back open, ready to blast this beast back to hell. He fired four bullets into the creature, enough to stop most animals in their tracks, but the tri-legged monstrosity seemed unaffected. It simply hissed like a snake then took off running. Or rather, it took off hopping. It covered over seventy-five feet in just three hops and disappeared into the night. The extra leg clearly gave it some sort of athletic advantage.

McDaniel called the police as soon as he knew the creature was gone and his family was safe. The authorities arrived and though they could not find the monster, they found evidence of it. They discovered scratch marks on the McDaniel door and clawed foot prints in the mud. Two of the footprints were the same size, while a third was significantly smaller. This suggested that the creature's third leg was oddly proportioned to the other two.

When the cops checked on the neighbours to see if they had seen anything, they heard young Greg's story. It seemed like there were two possibilities: either the McDaniel family had collaborated with the ten-year-old next door to fabricate a three-legged monster attack, or there was some truth in what they were saying. With the tripod terror having fled the scene, though, it seemed like the case was closed. All they could do was hope that it wouldn't return.

On May 6, Henry McDaniel was rudely awoken at 3.00 AM by the barking of neighbourhood dogs. He wondered what could have gotten the pooches so worked up. Then he remembered the monster. He jumped out of bed and grabbed his gun. He ran to the door and threw it open. Over his property, next to some train tracks, he saw the tri-pedal beast once again. This time, though, he didn't open fire. The monster either didn't notice Henry, or just didn't care that he was there. If the creature *did* notice Henry, luckily it seemed to be harbouring no vendetta about being shot by him just weeks ago. The creature was just making its way along the tracks, in no great rush. Henry watched it until it had meandered out of sight.

As soon as the sun was up, Henry started to tell everyone he could about the monster he had now seen twice. Word spread fast, as word of encounters with strange creatures tend to. Soon locals started searching the woods, hoping for a glimpse of what was now being called the Enfield Horror. Even monster tourists from out of town started travelling in. Monster fever reached such high proportions that the local sheriff had to warn Henry McDaniel that if he didn't stop talking about it, he'd have to arrest him or even have him sectioned.

Henry calmed down with his tales of a short grey beast, but it was too late. Enfield was swarmed with wannabe monsterologists. But did any of them find what they were looking for? A man who worked for the local radio station claimed that he and three friends had spotted the creature close to an abandoned building not far from the McDaniel house. He said that it was too dark outside and it moved too quickly to get a good look at it. All they could make out was that it was around five feet tall, grey, and was slouched over. The number of legs it had was not mentioned. He claimed to have captured the strange noises the beast made on a small tape recorder as it ran, or hopped, away at record speeds. Similar sounds were reportedly heard by a cryptozoologist who came to investigate.

In the end, though, more people were arrested for tramping through the Enfield woods armed with guns and cameras, determined to shoot the monster in one way or another, than ever actually saw it. As time went on, residents of Enfield would claim that they thought the whole thing was a hoax. Business owners would complain that the brief flap of monster mania didn't even drum up much business for them. A hurtful poem about Henry McDaniel and the monster was even composed. I could find no surviving document of this poem, but I can't imagine it was Oscar Wilde (or even Aleister Crowley) material. After the dust had settled, Henry became one more person in the long list of people who had seen something strange, spoke about it, and ended up wishing they hadn't.

Theories on what the monster actually was, if it was indeed real, ranged from an alien, a creature from another dimension, and even a mad scientists' escaped biological experiment gone wrong. Whatever it was, the Enfield Monster became another creature who appeared for a short period of time then vanished off the face of the Earth.

You might be thinking to yourself; "Why have I never heard of this three-legged, child-attacking, bullet-absorbing, great-distance-hopping cryptid before?" Some might say that the reason the story of the Enfield Horror isn't more well known is because of how few people saw it and the belief that the whole thing may have been a hoax. We've covered plenty of strange beasts and entities in this book already that you could say the same thing about, and they've still slipped into legend.

The real reason may be because this is not the most well-known weird story from an Enfield. The most well-known story doesn't take place in Enfield, Illinois, though; it takes place in Enfield, England. In 1977, a house in Enfield became the setting for quite possibly the most famous poltergeist inhabitation in history. In the years since, it has been the subject of countless books, TV specials, and documentaries. It was even the basis for the second instalment in the popular horror movie franchise *The Conjuring*. Due to this, any attempt to research a strange event in Enfield will inevitably turn up results for the Enfield Poltergeist and not our three-legged friend.

Could the Enfield Horror take its rightful place at the cryptid table if it was just easier to find? Just like the Flatwoods Monster was given the nickname Braxxie, is it time for a rebrand? Could a catchier name finally earn the Enfield Monster the respect it deserves and differentiate it from the English poltergeist? Personally, I'd like to suggest 'The Illinois Tri-legged Hopper'. Let's make it happen, people!

OUT OF THIS WORLD PANCAKES

After a person meets an extraterrestrial, sometimes they are left with a gift.

Usually this gift is a patch of missing memory, a mild case of radiation sickness, or a touch of anxiety, but sometimes the gift is a little more thoughtful and physical. Some have claimed to have received actual materials and technology from alien beings. These items, allegedly from inside UFOs and totally out of this world, are usually found to be entirely possible to create on Earth. Sceptics say this is proof that these items are forgeries and hoaxes, while believers say it's perfectly reasonable to assume that extraterrestrials would be working with the same compounds and elements as we are. Either way, receiving a physical item from an alien is certainly an interesting concept and adds a whole new level to a person's close encounter.

Sometimes, though, the gift they give is stranger than memory loss or a supposed metamaterial. Sometimes the gift is so bizarre that you cannot help but believe it. For one man in Eagle River, Wisconsin, that gift was pancakes.

At 11.00 AM on April 18, 1961, sixty-year-old plumber and poultry farmer Joseph Simonton was sitting down for a late breakfast. His most important meal of the day was interrupted by a ruckus coming from outside. Fearing an escape attempt by the chickens, he rushed to the window. What he saw was not a feathery jailbreak. What he saw was a chrome flying saucer hovering over his backyard. Simonton watched in awe as it slowly descended and landed.

Some people may have feared an impending abduction or even a full blown invasion, but like most farmers, Joseph was a practical man. He wasn't afraid of this UFO that had parked on his property; he was just curious about it. He stepped out into his backyard to investigate. As he approached the four metre tall, ten metre wide silvery saucer, a hatch opened on its hull. Joseph wandered on over to have a good old look inside.

What he saw inside the craft was not alien penguins, extraterrestrial jelly or intergalactic goblins. It wasn't even small grey guys with big heads and black eyes. It was three entirely normal-looking olive-skinned men in tight blue jumpsuits with turtle necks and helmets on their heads. Joseph said they looked Italian. Whether they had the accent to match is unknown, as these ufonauts stayed entirely silent.

This muteness seemed not to be by choice, though, as they did try to communicate with Joseph, they just couldn't do it verbally. One of the craft's occupants leaned out the hatch and silently greeted Joseph. This Italien (Italian alien) was holding a large jug and was motioning with it. It didn't take Joseph long to deduce that his new tight-clothed friend wanted him to fill the jug. With water, he assumed. Being the kind, salt-of-the-earth man that he was, Joseph obliged.

He took the jug to a nearby pump and filled it with some nice clean H_2O. He lugged it back to the saucer and handed it to the patiently waiting humanoid. As he handed the jug back, Joseph got a better look at the interior of the UFO. One of the three saucer people was busy working on some sort of dashboard. The second looked like it was getting ready to cook over a grill that curiously had no flame. The third took the newly filled water jug back, and gave Joseph a little treat for his troubles. He handed him four items that Joseph could only compare to pancakes. They were each four to five inches long, oval, crispy and full of tiny holes.

As Joseph stared at these odd objects, the hatch closed, the UFO rose into the sky, and it flew off. He looked back to the four pancakes, and they did not exactly look appetising. They looked like, and I hope I don't offend any extraterrestrial chefs that may be reading, giant scabs. He decided, though, that it would be rude to not at least try one. He took a bite and…it wasn't great. Joseph described it as tasting like cardboard. The aliens should maybe have offered him some syrup to go along with them.

Joseph would have been quite happy to have left the whole strange situation there, but neighbours actually saw the UFO take off and phoned the Air Force. When they came to investigate and asked Joseph if had seen anything unusual, they were quite surprised to hear that not only had he seen the aluminium domed craft, not only had it landed on his farm, not only had he met its occupants, but he had received some crunchy pancakes from them.

The Air Force decided that this was out of their wheelhouse. They called in Project Blue Book. This organisation was set up by the US government to debunk these sorts of encounters, but its head, the legendary J. Allen Hynek, would become a true believer in the UFO phenomenon. Hynek interviewed Joseph and believed his story. He was won over by his sincerity and Joseph's insistence that he knew no one would believe him, but he didn't care. He wasn't going to lie about his experience.

So what happened to the three uneaten pancakes? One was given to a local judge who also believed Joseph's story. Another was given to Hynek and I'm sure was kept as prized possession. The final alien pancake was taken by the Food and Drug Administration for testing.

These tests concluded that the ingredients used to make the pancakes were entirely terrestrial in origin. This came as a blow to those who were anticipating pancake batter mixed from substances from another galaxy, and is likely why the case was quickly dismissed. The story hit the news media and they reported it with the level of seriousness you'd expect them to. A defeated Joseph would later say, "If it happened again, I don't think I'd tell anybody about it."

Did Joseph really receive some pancakes from three aliens hailing from Planet Italy? As silly as the concept sounds, maybe!

Could the commotion he heard that alerted him to the silver saucers presence have been the sound of it breaking down or malfunctioning? Was it even a simple case of the craft running out of energy? Did they request water from him because they use this as a fuel source? If you'll remember, the Men in Black alluded to using sea water for a similar reason to Albert Bender. Maybe sea water and fresh water can both be used. Maybe it's like diesel and petrol.

As for the pancakes, is it so crazy to believe that they would be made from Earthly ingredients? If these aliens were here to investigate our planet, wouldn't they use what they found here as a food source rather than packing an entire pantry into their relatively small craft? Maybe the eggs in the pancakes were from Joseph's own chickens!

Joseph Simonton was not a man given to flights of fancy and tall tales. In fact, the judge who was given one of the pancakes knew Joseph and vouched for his integrity, honestly, and strength of character. He had nothing to gain from his story. He simply told his story because he felt it was the right thing to do.

Sadly, in telling his story, he was subjected to ridicule by many. Ridicule to the extent that he regretted ever speaking up in the first place. It's this

146

reaction that means we may never know if Joseph's mute friends ever came back for seconds.

BATSQUATCH: THE FLYING BIGFOOT

I doubt anyone reading this book *isn't* familiar with Bigfoot.

It is possibly the most famous cryptid of all time, alongside Nessie and Mothman. Much like these other celebrity monsters, though, its existence is hotly debated. Many scientifically minded people say the possibility of an entire species of hairy humanoids living in the woods of the world and staying entirely undiscovered is slim to impossible. This sceptical belief is backed up by the fact that any supposed proof of a Bigfoot (footprints, hair samples, bowel movements, blurry photos) when examined by professionals is usually determined to be inconclusive at best or a total hoax at worst.

Despite this, every year people come forward claiming to have seen an unclassified, tall, hairy, bipedal creature lumbering through the forest. And these reports come from the world over. Bigfoot, or Sasquatch, comes from North America. The Yeti, or the Abominable Snowman, comes from Asia. Even Scotland has the Grey Man on the Ben MacDhui mountain range. From around the world, reports come in of people seeing very similar creatures, but these creatures leave no trace or proof of their existence. Because of this, some have put forward the theory that Bigfoot isn't of this Earth.

Some people are adamant that Bigfoot and his kin are creatures from another dimension who slip in and out of our world without leaving a trace. Whether these hairy visitors can do this at will, or if it's something that happens to them entirely at random, is up for debate. Either way, the idea that this famous cryptid can pop in and out of our world answers a lot of questions that sceptics have. Why has a Bigfoot never been found? Why can we find no evidence of one? They just teleported back to their own dimension before they left any trace: simple!

Even with this very basic interdimensional explanation, sceptics still have a hard time coming to terms with the existence of Bigfoot. If they struggle with believing that a hairy humanoid exists, imagine how they would feel about Bigfoot if you attached a pair of giant bat wings to him.

On a night in April 1994, an eighteen-year-old named Brian Canfield was driving on a country road near Mount Rainier in Pierce County, Washington. While driving, his truck suddenly and seemingly without reason died. The engine stopped and the dashboard lights cut off, but the headlights stayed on. It was the headlights that would reveal to him a creature beyond his wildest imagination.

First Brian saw feet descending into the beam of light. These were no human feet though, they looked like they belonged to a bird. They had claws and talons, but these feet were far too big to belong to any known bird species. The feet landed on the road with the sound of flapping wings, and Brian got a look at the animal they belonged to. This was no animal he was familiar with. It was humanoid, and stood on two legs. It was over nine feet tall. It was covered in dark fur and vaguely resembled some sort of ape or bear. It had yellow eyes, a dog-like muzzle, and long, sharp teeth. Perhaps most shockingly of all, though: on its back was a giant pair of leathery bat wings. It landed with such force that dust and stones were launched very cinematically into the air around it.

Brian was frozen, white-knuckled hands gripping the useless steering wheel. The creature that looked like a winged Bigfoot stared at him and the truck. Minutes passed while Brian stayed as still as he could, fearing any sudden movement might provoke an attack from the creature. "I've got to stay still," he thought, working under the assumption that this beast's vision may be based on movement like the T-rex from *Jurassic Park*, which was released the previous summer.

The Batsquatch stayed just as still, keeping a close eye on Brian. Suddenly, its long furry fingers twitched. Then the wings unfolded back out from its broad shoulders, revealing its massive wingspan once more. Brian said that, when unfolded, the wings were almost as wide as the road itself. The wings began to flap, and the power behind them was so great that the truck started to sway. The Batsquatch rose into the air, fixed Brian with one final look, then took off towards Mount Rainier.

Mount Rainier, it is worth noting, already had some weird history attached to it. In 1947, the pilot Kenneth Arnold saw nine UFOs over the mountain during a flight. It was his description of these objects that first inspired the term "flying saucer". While it may be a stretch to claim that these craft were piloted by Batsquatches (why would they need flying saucers if they already had wings?), it is certainly a fun scene to imagine!

Brian watched the creature fly off and disappear into the darkness of the night, shocked and unsure of what to do next. A few minutes after the creature took off towards the mountain, his truck came back to life. As mysteriously as it had broken down, it began to work again, and Brian was able (and glad) to drive away from the spot he encountered the bizarre hairy flying creature.

Brian arrived home and quickly woke his parents. He told his father to grab a camera and a gun and to follow him. His parents were baffled but knew something had obviously happened to their son. As they quickly got dressed,

Brian frantically told them that while he was driving his truck had died and a flying sasquatch had landed in front of him.

If this was a horror movie, the parents would likely have told Brian he had imagined the whole thing and/or laughed at him. But they could see that their son was shaking. His hair was standing on end. He was pale. Something *had* happened on that country road. The family went to a nearby house and woke their neighbour. He was a man familiar with the woods, and Brian told him the story. He was just as baffled as Brian and his family. They all decided to drive out to where the encounter had taken place to see if any evidence had been left. They found nothing.

Brian's story was told by journalist C.R. Roberts in the May 1994 edition of Tacoma's *News Tribune*. Roberts was convinced that Brian had seen something strange that night due to the boy's sincerity and the fact that he wasn't a fan of heavy metal music and that he'd never played Dungeons & Dragons — the two factors that usually cast doubt on any cryptid witness, but without which make said witness frightfully boring.

Roberts also shared that Brian had begun to get some fun poked at him in high school over his story, and shared a drawing of the creature that a classmate had sketched based on Brian's description. It included the fact that some had dubbed the creature Batsquatch.

This was not the only time a flying sasquatch has been reported.

In 2009, in California, several hikers reported seeing a huge, hair-covered creature flying out of a crevice on Mt. Shasta. They claimed the creature had leathery bat wings that spanned fifty feet. One witness claimed it was not dissimilar to a flying fox bat, the largest bat species in the world. Some sceptics have claimed this is what these hikers saw, but the flying fox is native to Asia and has a wingspan of only five to six feet.

In 2011, in Ohio, a man was walking his dog when he saw something in the sky. It was at least nine feet tall, it had dark fur with a blue tinge, glowing eyes and bat wings.

There are many short accounts of people seeing a strange Bigfoot-like entity flying through the sky with massive bat wings. They continue to this day and some even predate Brian Canfield's encounter in 1994.

While it's hard to point to the exact origin of Batsquatch, some believe it may be connected to the 1980 eruption of Mount St. Helens.

When St. Helens started belching smoke into the sky and spewing molten lava, some speculate that it also released something else. When the volcano became active again after 140 years of laying dormant, people in the area around St. Helens started reporting sightings of a large winged creature.

The creature appeared shortly before the first earthquakes that signalled something was afoot in the volcano, and continued until after the actual eruption. This has led some to theorise that Batsquatch was actually released by the volcano coming to life. Could the volcano erupting have freed Batsquatch from a subterranean prison of sorts? Could the initial earthquakes have shaken free vast quantities of rock that kept the monster underground?

Believers in the Hollow Earth Theory claim that Batsquatch is a resident of the titular Hollow Earth, and the eruption of Mount St. Helens created some sort of entrance to our world. Hollow Earth is a theory that the Earth is, you guessed it, hollow. In this hollow space, an entirely different world exists. A world that houses strange creatures and animals that are totally unheard of on our exterior Earth.

Some entrances to Hollow Earth can be found, it is said, in large cave systems and deep caverns where man can barely get to. Some people throughout history have claimed to have found these entrances and even taken brief trips into the Hollow Earth. Could the events of Mount St. Helens have ripped a new hole into Hollow Earth, and did Batsquatch use this to escape through? Could a whole family of them have flown out and spread across America, being sporadically spotted by locals in whatever area they decide to take up residency?

And what of the original flying saucers spotted by Kenneth Arnold over Mount Rainier? Could some UFOs be the vehicles that advanced beings use to travel from the Hollow Earth into our world? Could these craft not have come from outer space, but inner Earth? Could they not be extraterrestrial, but intraterrestrial?

The fact that Batsquatch appeared around the eruption of a volcano is eerily similar to another cryptid who appeared before a disaster. In Point Pleasant, West Virginia, on December 15, 1967, the Silver Bridge collapsed into the Ohio River, killing forty-six people. For months before this tragedy, residents of Point Pleasant reported seeing a large dark bipedal humanoid with glowing red eyes and huge wings: the Mothman.

Mothman appeared as if from nowhere and began terrifying locals, and even causing some physical harm. Mothman never actually attacked anyone, but just being in its presence and getting hit with its red eyed gaze would cause skin burns, conjunctivitis, and illness. Some believe that Mothman appearing was connected to the Silver Bridge collapse.

Some believe that Mothman was a messenger, a creature from another dimension sent to warn the residents of Point Pleasant of the impending disaster. Sadly, it lacked the communication skills necessary to get this across, and just gave people sunburn. Others say that Mothman is a harbinger of doom. They believe that Mothman wasn't there to warn of the disaster, but simply to enjoy it. Some go so far as to say that Mothman appearing even caused the collapse. Because of this, many believe that the sighting of a cryptid is a very bad omen indeed.

Batsquatch could be an actual animal, maybe an even rarer cousin to the flightless Bigfoot, though the fact it seemed to be able to stop a car working without even touching it doesn't point towards it. Batsquatch could be a strange and unknown creature from inside our own Earth that possesses eerie powers. It could even be a creature from another reality or dimension, sent to warn us of impending doom — or just to revel in it.

When Mothman struck the town of Point Pleasant, sightings of a giant anthropomorphic insect wasn't the only strange thing going on. People reported a spike in poltergeist activity, UFOs were seen with shocking frequency, and creepy men in black suits stalked the town asking locals weird questions. It seemed that when Mothman ripped through from another dimension, ghosts, aliens, and the Men in Black followed it. Some theorise that even the injuries that people sustained after seeing this winged terror point to interdimensional evidence. The injuries described are similar to those exposed to radiation. Some speculate that Mothman and other cryptids give off some sort of radioactive byproduct that is caused by them being in our reality.

What does this have to do with Batsquatch? Very little research has been done into how the witnesses felt afterwards and if anything else strange had been happening in the area around the same time as a sighting. I would not be surprised if Brian Canfield received a knock on the door a few days after his encounter, while nursing a bad case of pink eye, and was greeted by three tall men in black suits.

As an interesting side note — southeast Asia has its own cryptid that is quite similar to the Batsquatch in description: the Ahool.

In 1925, Dr Ernest Bartels was exploring a waterfall on the Salek Mountains in the jungles of Java when something that looked like a giant bat flew over his head. This wasn't a giant bat like the aforementioned flying fox. It was much bigger, with a wingspan that could have been as large as twenty-eight feet. It also didn't look like any known bat. It had the leathery wings of a bat (albeit giant), but its body was closer to that of a primate. Its face was something like a cross of the two animals it seemed to embody, part bat and part ape. It was covered in grey fur and had claws on its forearms and talons on its feet. Although it made no attempt to attack Bartels, he was sure this animal was a carnivore. This was the first reported sighting of the Ahool.

It wasn't until two years later that the Ahool would get its name however. In 1927, Bartels was in his hut close to a river in Java late at night. He was trying to drift off to sleep when a sound woke him straight back up. Bartels was used to the sounds that would come from the jungle, but what he heard that night was unlike anything he had ever heard before. A sound he was sure could only have come from the giant bat creature he had seen two years prior. A sound that Bartels would later mimic as "A hool!"

Since Bartels brought this strange creature to light, it has been sighted all over the jungles of Java. Many even came forward with experiences that pre-dated Bartels' waterfall encounter. Maybe another passageway exists in this jungle; though, whether this passageway is a physical one to the Hollow Earth or a metaphysical one to another dimension is unknown.

THE FINNISH SPACE GNOME

The motivations of unknowable beings and entities are unsurprisingly often mysterious.

Why are they here? What do they want? Why am I seeing them; is it accidental or by choice? Perhaps if we could know the answer to even one of these questions we'd have a better idea of how to react when we're suddenly face-to-face with a creature from another world. Do we shake their hand/tentacle/claw? Do we offer them a refreshing beverage? Do we take them to our leader? As it stands, we currently have three popular reactions: run, try to kill it, or stand dumbfounded until the situation has played itself out. Two Finnish men chose the latter in their own bizarre encounter, and it may not have been the best option.

On January 7, 1970, Aarno Heinonen and Esko Viljo were out skiing in the woods near the Finnish village of Imjarvi. Night was beginning to fall, and the men paused in a clearing to catch their breath. Perhaps if they had just pushed on, they would have been spared the bizarre event they were about to be subjected to.

The men were enjoying a quick look at the stars that were starting to appear overhead when they heard a buzzing sound. The men were confused, seeing no source of the sound. This is when the source appeared over the top of the trees that surrounded them. The stars, as nice as they were, quickly became an afterthought.

At first they only saw a cloud of red smoke with a light shining out from within it. As this red smoke got closer to the men, they realised that the light was coming from a solid object. The solid object was a metallic saucer that was roughly nine feet wide. It had a dome on top and three small half-spheres around the rim of the underside. The men watched dumbfounded as the craft within the smoke crested the treeline and hovered in the air over the centre of the clearing. It was at this point that Aarno and Esko realised that the saucer was producing the mist that surrounded it in small scarlett puffs. After briefly floating motionless, the craft began to descend.

The UFO stopped its descent about ten feet above the snow covered ground. It was so close that Aarno would later claim that he could have reached out and touched the craft with his ski pole. An opening appeared in the centre of the bottom of the craft and a beam of light shone down. A puff of red mist blasted down, briefly covering the beam of light. When the mist cleared, a figure now stood in the light. The figure was humanoid, but only three feet tall. It wore a one-piece green outfit, with darker green boots and white gloves. On its head it wore a silver conical hat or helmet. Its face was almost human, but very pale and the skin looked like wax. Its nose looked larger and more hooked than a human nose, and its ears were small and high up on its head. The small humanoid held something in its gloved hands: a black box.

The men stared at this strange small "man" and wondered what it was and what it wanted. It silently turned towards Aarno and pointed the black box at him. A bright light blasted out of it and struck Aarno. Red mist descended from the craft, enveloping the creature and surrounding the men. Visibility was tough; the men couldn't even see each other, but they saw sparks coming from where the creature stood. The light beam it stood in shot upwards, back into the craft. The cloud dissipated, and when it did there was no craft and no creature.

The men stood for several minutes in shock before deciding it was time to head home. As they went to leave the clearing, Aarno suddenly realised that he was basically paralysed on the entire right side of his body. His leg would not support his weight. Aarno's mobility was affected so badly that he even had to remove his skis and leave them behind in the clearing. Esko supported his friend and all but carried him home.

The two men arrived at Aarno's mother's home sometime later. When Mrs Heinonen let the pair in, she knew something was wrong. Not only was Esko holding her son up, but Esko's face was red and swollen.

Before the men could tell Mrs Heinonen what had happened to them out in the woods, Aarno was overcome by the urge to vomit. Being a very polite young man and not wanting to ruin her bathroom, he managed to hobble his way back outside and evacuate his stomach contents there.

While outside, he realised that he desperately needed to urinate. Having no time to return inside, and being quite secluded, he did it then and there. He began the process and (**warning:** if you are enjoying a damn fine cup of coffee while reading this chapter, please finish it before continuing) his urine was the colour and consistency of thick espresso. It melted through the snow and ice on the ground like xenomorph blood through the hull of a spaceship. When he returned to the house, his head and joints ached.

Esko decided that his friend required immediate medical attention, but Mrs Heinonen didn't have a phone. Esko hurried to a neighbour's house 600 metres away, who thankfully let him use their telephone. The first two doctors he called couldn't see the pair, but the third, Dr Kajanoja, said he could see them at the local hospital in one hour's time. This was good news, but there was a major problem: the location was quite a bit away and neither Esko, Aarno, or his mother had a car. Luckily, the helpful neighbour owned a car as well as a phone and offered to drive them.

Dr Kajanoja saw the men as promised and quickly realised that they were in a state of shock. By the swollen red skin, aching heads and joints, and pitch black whizz, the doctor speculated that the men had radiation poisoning, though he lacked the equipment to prove it. He prescribed the men painkillers and sleeping pills, assuring them that their symptoms would be gone in a week or so. If this was a normal illness, the doctor would probably have been right.

Weeks passed and the men still had health problems. Though Aarno regained the use of his right side, he struggled to maintain balance while standing up. The blast from the black box had also affected his memory somehow, with it becoming very poor after the encounter. For months after being hit with the light beam, his pee remained a deep black. Esko, who only seemed to have suffered some mild skin burns, also had health problems. He suffered from intense headaches and eye problems. Interestingly, as word of the men's encounter spread, people would visit the clearing where they had seen the UFO and small humanoid. Reportedly, many of the people who went to this area would fall ill. Was there some sort of leftover radiation from whatever shot out of the black box?

The men would slowly heal. Balance was regained, memory was restored, and pee was returned to its classic yellow colour. Although the story that Aarno and Esko had to tell was certainly interesting, no solid evidence could be found to support it. Sure, the men had visible problems after their encounter, but their word was all investigators really had to go on.

To support the men's story, it was discovered that earlier in the same day that the men saw the strange craft and little humanoid, a farmer's wife had seen a strange light in the sky in the direction of Imjarvi. Perhaps the same craft, or a scout ship? This backed up the men's story, but what made investigators, family, friends, medical professionals, and town locals believe that something weird had truly happened, was the men's reputations. No one believed that they would lie about such a thing.

This, coupled with their injuries made for a compelling story. Even if the men *were* lying about the craft and creature, no one was sure how else they could have possibly ended up with what seemed to be radiation poisoning. The whole thing was just too weird, and had to be believed. And that is the end of that story.

Or is it?

It seemed that the world of the weirder than weird wasn't quite done with Aarno Heinonen just yet. Between January 1970 and August 1972, Aarno would claim to have seen twenty-three more UFOs. But that's not all; he even claimed to have met what he assumed to be one of the occupants of the craft. This occupant was no short humanoid in a pointy hat this time, though; it was an extremely attractive human-looking woman. She had long hair, blue eyes, and wore a yellow pantsuit (possibly predicting the fashion for the rest of the 70s). She had teeth that were twice as wide as normal human ones. She usually floated or levitated above the ground, but when she did walk she did so without using her knees. This explains why levitation was the preferred mode of movement.

She communicated with Aarno not verbally, but telepathically. Her big teeth possibly made normal conversation difficult. In these meetings, she held a small metal sphere that had three antennae poking out of it. On one occasion, she left their meeting by pulling on one of the ball's antennas and flying straight up into the air. The function of the other two antennae are unknown.

Their meetings typically only lasted minutes, but she managed to share a great deal of information with him. She told Aarno that she came from a green land (not to be confused with Greenland) on the other side of the Milky Way, that three different species of extraterrestrials had visited the location near Imjarvi, and that she was 180 years old. She looked great for her age!

Sadly, these stories of multiple UFO sightings and bodacious levitating space women who communicate telepathically in fluent Finnish might be the reason little research was done into the case further down the line. Much like when Albert Bender claimed to have been teleported to a secret base in Antarctica by the Men in Black, many people thought this was just too silly and unbelievable. Because of this, some researchers have looked back at the initial encounter in the clearing and dismissed it outright. People seeing UFOs multiple times throughout their lives, and even being contacted again and again by extraterrestrial beings, is nothing new in the world of ufology.

But even if we discount everything after the encounter in the clearing, what happened in the forest outside of Imjarvi to Aarno and Esko is still well worth investigating. Something very strange did happen to these men. Something that had a lasting effect not just physically, but psychologically.

But what did they experience in the clearing that evening? A craft and a creature from another world or dimension? What was the black box, and what did it shoot at Aarno? Was it a weapon? It certainly harmed Aarno, and even hurt Esko, though he wasn't the target of the light beam. Why did the strange small creature decide to blast the men with what may have been a deadly radioactive weapon? Why did it even appear to them in the first place?

When we think about the description of the creature that beamed down from the craft, it may hold some answers. The men described the creature as being very short, wearing green clothes and a pointy silver hat, and having a hooked nose. It sounds very similar to a creature out of folklore. It sounds like a gnome.

Finland has a rich history of folklore which includes fey creatures like gnomes, trolls, pixies, and elves. These kinds of creatures have been reported the world over throughout history, but many of these reports when viewed through a modern lens sound very similar to more recent extraterrestrial encounters. Could these gnome aliens have been visiting Earth for millenia, laying the basis for the folklore myth?

In many of these stories, the best way to win the favour of a fey creature is to give it an offering. Could this creature have beamed down to Aarno and Esko expecting a gift, but when the men were too dumbfounded to give it anything, it blasted Aarno with its radioactive box as punishment, accidently catching Esko in the crossfire? They say that failing to offer something to a fey creature will result in bad luck, and I'd say a healthy dose of radiation poisoning fits that description.

If you should ever be out in the woods and stumble across a strange beast that seems to have jumped right out of a fairytale and you don't want to end up with black pee, just give it something. Empty your pockets. Gum, handkerchief, train ticket, wallet, phone, whatever. It's mugging rules at this point.

THE CREEPIEST CHILDREN: BLACK-EYED KIDS

Kids are creepy.

I say this not in an attempt to be unpleasant or insulting; I say it as a simple fact. In fact, this may be one of the few "facts" in this book that cannot be debated. Whether they are appearing in horror movies announcing the arrival of poltergeists, or whether they're in your living room talking to their "invisible friend" who is actually a demon, children have the ability to be creepier than any entity we've covered in this book.

To be fair to children, though, they don't *know* they're being creepy. In horror movies, they are used to innocently react to paranormal happenings they simply don't understand. In real life, they have no idea that their new friend Steve that only they can see is really Zazzukkok from the Dimension of Eternal Torture and that the house is going to need blessed by a priest next week. Creepy as they can be, they don't do it on purpose.

At least, *human* children don't. There is another type of child that looks almost human, but is anything but. This type of child seems to thrive on being as creepy as possible. First, they approach you at night, at a time when any child their age should be safely at home or in bed. Then you notice their impossibly pale, ghost-like skin. Then they speak to you, asking for a ride home or entrance into your house. You know you shouldn't let them, but the way they talk seems to have an almost hypnotic quality that bends your mind to their will. Finally, you notice their most striking feature: their eyes have no colour. Where a pupil and the whites of the eyes should be, there is only total darkness.

The legend of the Black-eyed Kids began one evening in Texas in 1995 when Brian Bethel was sitting in his truck in a cinema car park. He was using the light from the cinema sign to write a cheque when suddenly his concentration was broken by a knock at the window. When he looked up, he didn't see a cop asking him what he was doing or a car park attendant asking him to move along; he saw two kids.

The pair were between nine and twelve years old and both wore hoodies, which partially obscured their faces. It was night, and it was unusual for these kids to be out and about, so Brian thought maybe they needed help and rolled down his window. As soon as the glass that separated Brian from the two kids was removed, he felt an unexpected and intense feeling of fear.

One of the kids spoke, while the second stayed quiet. The young man who spoke to Brian was olive skinned and had curly hair. He asked if he and his friend could have a lift to his mother's house. They wanted to see the *Mortal Kombat* film (they might be creepy, but they have good taste!), but had forgotten to take any money. They needed to go home, pick up some cash, then return and buy a ticket.

Brian thought this was unusual, but harmless. As the curly-haired kid spoke, though, the feeling of fear that he felt increased. He couldn't figure it out — why was he so afraid of these children? The curly-haired kid kept speaking to Brian, saying things like "It wouldn't take long" and "we're just two little kids." Red flags were starting to show.

At this point Brian glanced up at the cinema marquee. The final showing of *Mortal Kombat* had already started. Even if the kids lived nearby, they'd have missed most of the film by the time they got back. How would they possibly know what was going on? They wouldn't even know why Scorpion and Sub-Zero were fighting!

When Brian looked back towards the kids, he suddenly noticed that both of them were staring at him with pitch black eyes. He tried his best to stay calm, or at the very least *appear* calm. He started to blurt out any random reasons he could think of for why he couldn't give the pair a lift. He started rolling the window back up as quickly as his arm could rotate and began to reverse the car.

Even with the car in motion, the curly-haired kid followed and banged on the window. He shouted, "We can't come in unless you tell us it's okay! Let us in!" "That's going to be a hard pass," thought Brian. He drove out of a primal fear that told him to get away from these boys as quickly as he possibly could, even if it meant destroying his car in the process.

When he was safely out of the cinema car park, he looked in his rear view mirror. The two kids were gone. They could not have run away in the time it took Brian to speed out of there, and there were no other cars for them to be hiding behind. They had simply vanished.

Brian wrote down his story and shared it through an email list. Though his story was initially only for his friends and colleagues to read, it was quickly shared and forwarded throughout the internet. Brian's story had gone viral in a time before that was even really a thing. People were captivated by his story about the short encounter he had with two creepy children in a cinema car park. The paranormal community of the early internet even came up with a term for the two boys. They were dubbed Black-eyed Kids, or BEKs for short.

The reason that Brian's story went so far wasn't just because it was a true story. It wasn't even just because it tapped into all our fears of children. It was because people started sharing their own encounters with Black-eyed Kids.

A BEK report from 2015, almost twenty years after Brian's encounter in the cinema car park, would become one of the most famous. It would also add to the lore of the BEKs, hinting at even more powers, giving an idea as to what might happen if you do invite these kids into your home, and even giving a clue towards the possible origin of the Black-eyed Kids.

In rural Vermont, an unnamed woman was awoken from her sleep at around 2.00 AM by a loud banging at her front door. The woman was concerned, as two o'clock in the morning was a very unexpected time to get visitors. She stealthily looked out the window and saw two figures standing at the door. It was too dark to make out any details, but she was alarmed. She woke her husband (who was evidently a deep sleeper) and told him about the knocking and the two people at the door.

Her husband was not as concerned as she was with this situation that could easily be the opening scene to a horror movie. He walked on over and opened the front door. To their surprise, they found two kids standing on their doorstep. A girl and a boy, both around eight years old. Instantly, they were worried. Two children should not be out at this time of night. What's more, the temperature was low, there was snow on the ground, and these two kids weren't even wearing jackets. Had something happened? Was this pair in trouble? Did they need help?

The kids kept their heads down and seemed to be purposely trying not to make eye contact with the husband and wife. The woman described how her normal reaction to seeing two children on her doorstep in the middle of the night in the freezing cold would be to take them inside and help them however she could, but something in her head was telling her not to. Something inside of her knew not to let these kids inside her home.

After a moment of silence she asked the kids where their parents were. Without looking up they answered that they would be there soon. Right here may have been where many people would have slammed the door shut, locked every lock, pushed a couch up against it, and armed themselves until morning came. This woman's motherly instincts (or the kid's hypnotic powers) managed to override her fear and the voice in her head telling her not to let these children inside. She invited them in for some hot cocoa.

The kids sat in the living room with her husband while she made the drinks in the kitchen. She could hear her husband asking the kids various questions like if they were okay and if their parents' car had broken down. Each question would get the same answer: "Our parents will be here soon." If that isn't scary enough, the woman described the kids' tone as "sing-songy".

The woman noticed at this point that all four of her cats were in the kitchen with her. She described her cats as very friendly and that they would always go to meet guests. This time, though, they seemed to want to be anywhere but the living room. Not only did they seem reluctant to meet the new guests, they seemed scared. One even uncharacteristically hissed when the woman tried to pet it.

The woman finished making the cocoa and headed down the hallway for the living room, I'm sure as slowly as she could. As she approached, she realised that the one-sided conversation had stopped. When she entered the living room, she realised why. The kids sat silent and still on the couch, while her husband sat in a seat with his head in his hands. She asked him if he was okay and he said he was, he just felt dizzy all of a sudden. She handed the kids their cocoa, and they finally looked up. Their eyes were pitch black.

Before the woman could react, they asked if they could use the bathroom. She told them where it was, and they headed towards it…together. With the room clear, the woman asked her husband if he had seen their eyes. He had. They started to discuss who their parents could possibly be, when the man's nose started to bleed.

The woman rushed to the kitchen to get some tissues to stop the flow. The power cut out. The house was in total darkness. Her husband called to her from the living room. When she stepped back out into the hallway, she saw the dark silhouettes of the two kids in the lightless gloom. "Our parents are here," they said. They headed to the front door and, thankfully, left. The husband and wife ran to the window and saw a black car in the driveway. They saw the kids climbing in while standing by the car were two men. Two men wearing black suits. If you've been taking notes while reading this book, that description might have set off some alarm bells.

The man, perhaps feeling awkward, waved at the Men in Black. Predictably, they did not wave back. They aren't the politest bunch. The MIB got in the car, and drove off. Half an hour later, the power returned to the house. I imagine they kept the lights on for the rest of the night.

The BEKs grew to popularity in the days of the early internet after Brian Bethel's story spread around the world. In its wake, people recounted their own tales of childlike entities that both predate his 1995 story and that happened years later. Some have even shared strange stories without prior knowledge of the BEKs, only to have it connected to them after the online paranormal community points out the similarities.

A quick online search will reveal a vast list of BEK encounters from across the globe. Some are just short sightings, while others are pages-long, harrowing ordeals with these creepy kids. Brian's original story and the later one from

Vermont seem to be the most popular, but many exist and share the same themes; spooky children with pitch black eyes trying to gain entry to homes or vehicles with an almost hypnotic power of suggestion. But what are the Black-eyed Kids?

Theories run the gamut from ghosts to demons to vampires. Based on one story in particular, some believe them to be evil genies that will grant a wish in exchange for your soul. The clue to what they actually are may be in the Vermont story. The BEKs in this case repeatedly said that their parents were coming, and when they did arrive, they were Men in Black.

Could these BEKs have been speaking quite literally, and they are the children of the MIB? Could Black-eyed Kids grow up to be Men in Black? Could these kids be out training for their future careers in creeping out UFO researchers and witnesses? Should these younglings be renamed the Kids in Black (KIB) or the Men in Black Juniors (MIB jnrs)?

If this is the case, then the only way we're going to find out what the Black-eyed Kids truly are is if we first discover who or what the Men in Black are. And, perhaps most terrifyingly, how the MIB reproduce. I'll let someone else take the lead on researching that.

LIVING TROUSERS: THE FRESNO NIGHTCRAWLERS

There is no definitive proof of any paranormal phenomenon. Every photo of a UFO is blurry. Every video of Bigfoot is shaky and out of focus. Footage from alleged haunted houses that claim to show poltergeist activity tend to happen just out of frame, and when something flies into shot (thrown by a supposed ghost), sometimes we can see the fishing line attached to it.

There is a theory that any definite proof of the paranormal is quickly confiscated by shady government G-men working for a secret organisation that is dedicated to keeping the supernatural underwraps. Others say that the Men in Black themselves turn up to take or destroy any evidence, using their unexplainable abilities to know when someone has captured evidence of something out-of-this-world before they even tell or show anyone.

A third theory is that footage and pictures of UFOs, cryptids, ghosts, and more are always blurry and indecipherable *on purpose*. Some believe that creatures from other dimensions or realities have the ability to affect technology. When someone sees a flying saucer or a monster and whips out their phone (or Polaroid, depending on era) to try to snap a photo, the craft or beast in question activates some sort of power that throws the technology into disarray. Some people who have sworn to have seen something strange have said that their photos or footage have randomly and mysteriously been deleted shortly after. Sure, it's a convenient excuse to explain away a lack of evidence, but could absolutely everyone who has told a story like this be lying?

Every so often, though, a piece of evidence does slip through the fingers of government agents and demonic entities in black suits. When it comes to proof of the paranormal, there might actually be something: a piece of film that is readily available to view online. A short video that hit the web in the mid 2000s and baffled all who saw it. If you're wondering what it is, and why you haven't heard of it, the answer is simple: it's weird. It's nothing as simple as a lit-up disk flying through the sky or a furry humanoid taking a stroll through the forest. What we see on this film is what looks like two pairs of palazzo pants walking on their own accord.

In Fresno, California, in 2007, a man who is known only as Jose was woken up early in the morning by his dogs barking incessantly. Jose rose to see what had gotten them all worked up, and quickly deduced that they were barking at something in the garden. Jose quickly became concerned that there was an intruder, and that maybe this intruder would try to break in. Luckily, Jose had recently installed a security camera outside his home, so he flicked on the monitor to check out the situation. The camera was positioned on top of his garage and gave a wide, high view of the whole garden. If anyone was out there, Jose was sure they'd be caught on camera. He saw nothing but a dark, still yard, but still the dogs barked. They were convinced something was outside. Jose tried to explain to them that he had checked and no one was out there, but being dogs, they didn't follow what he was saying.

As they continued their howling, Jose started to worry that maybe someone was hiding outside, waiting until he went back to sleep to strike. Maybe they saw the light from the monitor being switched on through the blinds, knew they had awoken the homeowner, and were now hiding in a shrubbery waiting for them to let their guard down. He stared intently at the screen, looking for any sign of movement. He continued watching the night vision feed from the camera for a minute. Then two minutes. Then something strange happened. Jose caught his intruder.

Across Jose's garden walked a creature that was roughly a metre and a half tall. Most of its body was made up of two long legs. It seemed to be entirely white, or at the very least extremely pale. It had no visible arms, but it seemed like it had some sort of small head atop its legs. It walked in a fluid, flowing, almost surreal motion that was quite unusual to observe. At a glance, it looked like a pair of sentient trousers were having a stroll over Jose's property.

Jose was baffled. It was early in the morning, almost 1.00 AM; surely he was just overly tired and his mind was playing tricks on him. That was when *another* long legged creature walked into frame. It looked almost identical to the first, but slightly shorter.

What made this even weirder was that Jose's garden was surrounded by a fence. The bars on this fence were too close together for these creatures to have slipped through, as thin as they were. This meant they either jumped the fence with their long legs or simply materialised on the property. And where were they going? They walked into the top of the shot and walked out at the bottom.

It must have been this creature that set the dogs barking. But what were they? Could there be a logical explanation? Was it some sort of animal? It looked like no animal Jose had ever seen. Could it be a prank? Who would be playing it, and for what purpose? Who would make a pair of trousers walk across his garden knowing it would annoy his dogs and result in him watching his security camera? It didn't make any sense. As Jose pondered these possibilities, he decided he needed a second opinion.

Jose shook his brother awake, frantically telling him that he had to show him something. "Quick, wake up! There's trousers in the garden!" he yelled to his groggy and confused brother. He dragged him out of bed, sat him down in front of the monitor and rewound the footage. His brother was as shocked as he was, and he quickly ran outside to see if the creatures were still wandering around outside. They seemed to have vanished, but Jose and his brother did find small footprints in the grass that they deduced must have been made by the leg creatures.

They went back inside, watched the footage again and decided other people had to see this. It was here that they were struck with a problem. Jose's video security system was quite antiquated. It still recorded to VHS tape. And, when the tape was rewound, the camera would just record over the footage when used again. They had no way to copy the footage or even save it. This was when they decided that if they couldn't save the original footage, they could do the next best thing. They set up a camera and recorded it straight from the monitor. A recording of a recording.

With footage (of footage) of two out of this world creatures wandering across his garden, Jose began to think what to do with it. First, he showed some more family members to see what they thought and to see if they could think of a logical explanation for what was on screen. They were as confused as the brothers, and pressed him to phone the police. Jose decided against this, figuring that the police would have a hard time handcuffing creatures without arms. Instead, he contacted a local TV station. They sent a reporter to interview Jose and he showed her the footage.

The reporter was amazed by what she saw. The tape was rewound and rewatched many times. They decided she had to take a copy of it back to the station to broadcast to the community. Jose agreed to let her take away a copy, under the condition that he remain anonymous (which is why we only know him as Jose). The reporter agreed, and was able to make a copy of the recording of the recording of the original security camera footage.

The story and the video was broadcast on a local Spanish-speaking news programme. An extraterrestrial expert, Victor Camacho from MUFON (the Mutual UFO Network), was even contacted by the programme to confirm that the creatures on the tape were indeed aliens. Victor wasn't able to do this with any certainty, but he did take an interest in the case. He would go to speak to Jose at his home, and was convinced that at the very least that the man believed he had captured something out of the ordinary. If it was a hoax, Victor was sure that it wasn't Jose who had orchestrated it.

Amateur ufologists and cryptozoologists who saw the broadcast of Jose's tape tried to debunk it or confirm its validity. Much like Victor, they couldn't definitively prove anything. As the original recording was likely not of great visual quality, and the recording of the screen even worse, and the copy of this possibly degraded the quality *even further*, it was simply impossible to tell whether the leggy creatures walking across the garden were legit or a hoax.

A couple of years passed, and the video of the sentient white trousers taking a nighttime stroll faded into relative obscurity. The video made a small splash in the niche paranormal community on the internet when it was first uploaded online, but as time passed and no more information surfaced it became just one more of those videos you find at 3.00 AM after going down an unplanned supernatural video rabbithole on YouTube.

In 2010, Jose's video was given a resurgence, a second life, and a more mainstream platform. The paranormal investigation show *Fact or Faked* decided to look into Jose's video in the second episode of their first season. The *FoF* team travelled to Fresno, met with Jose, and tried to recreate and replicate his security camera video in an attempt to debunk it or prove that it was indeed something out of the ordinary. They positioned a camera in roughly the same location that the security camera had been, and waited for nightfall so the light conditions would be the same.

First, they tackled the claim that the creatures had simply been children walking across the lawn. Ignoring the obvious question of why two unsupervised kids would be walking around neighbourhood gardens at 1.00 AM, they put this theory to the test. They found a local child of roughly the same height as the creature in the video, dressed him all in white and had him walk through the frame. To the shock of no one, this piece of footage did not match up with Jose's. Not only did the child continue to have limbs other than legs when viewed on video, he simply did not walk in a manner that matched.

Next, they tackled the theory that the nightcrawlers were just puppets pulled along on a wire with a small mechanism to make their legs move. They constructed a rather horrifying model that looked like a blank mannequin head attached to two long and skinny life size doll legs. It was a look that was far more terrifying than our pale leggy friends! This still didn't match the original video, but when they tried again with a sheet draped over their model, it looked closer but still not quite right. At the end of their investigation they came to the groundbreaking and definite conclusion that they didn't know what the Fresno Nightcrawlers were. I'm glad we finally got our top men on the case.

While *Fact or Faked* may not have given us any new information on the Nightcrawlers, or manage to prove or disprove their existence, what the show *did* do was introduce a huge new audience to Jose's video. Suddenly, the Nightcrawlers were back in the limelight and reaching levels of mainstream popularity they never experienced the first time round, like Green Day when they released *American Idiot* (but no one was calling the Nightcrawlers sellouts). In an attempt to find out what the Nightcrawlers were, interested people began editing the video. It could be viewed online in slow motion, frame by frame, high contrast, low contrast, no contrast, noise turned up, noise turned down, infrared, colour corrected, and just about every other way you could imagine. But the creatures in the video remained unexplained.

As the Fresno Nightcrawlers video gained popularity and theories to both explain and debunk their existence flooded comment sections, the mostly-legged creatures reappeared. In March of 2011, a video hit YouTube that claimed to have been recorded in Yosemite National Park, not too far from Fresno. This video is allegedly from a security camera (again) that was put up by a retired couple living in the park. Apparently their property was being damaged at night by some sneaky person, so they set up a camera in order to catch them in the act. What they caught on the video wasn't some teenage vandal, though, it was something quite more unusual. Rather than call the authorities, the couple called the person who went on to upload the video to YouTube, as they knew he was interested in the paranormal. They thought he could help them get some answers.

In the video we see a darkened scene of a footpath and some trees. The camera is positioned in a jaunty angle, like it's ready to film a scene for *Battlefield Earth*. A few seconds pass, then our first Nightcrawler enters the frame from the left. It looks much like the creature from Jose's video, though this time it's clearer. Not only was this filmed digitally, but the copy given to the uploader was an actual file and not just a recording of a screen. Due to this jump in quality, we can see that there does indeed seem to be some sort of head on top of the long legs. We can also see that the creature could be wearing some sort of clothing. As it walks it looks like there is some type of fabric moving over its legs, like it's wearing white Nu-Metal style JNCO pants (long out of style by 2011).

179

It gets several steps into frame before a second Nightcrawler enters. It's further away from the camera, but it's clear that it's smaller than the first. Just like in Jose's video, there are two creatures, one tall and one shorter. They both also walked in a similar strange fashion like the ones in the original video. This led many to think that these were actually the same two Nightcrawlers that annoyed Jose's dogs when they took a walk on his lawn.

Though this video gave a clearer look at the creatures, it didn't convince everyone that they were real. Even some people who were convinced by Jose's video believed the Yosemite video was a fake. Theories ranged from these Nightcrawlers being a product of digital effects to impressive puppet work. Many believed that this video was made to capitalise on the original and make a couple of quick bucks. Less cynical people believed that it was more of a homage to the original, an attempt to add to the lore of the Nightcrawlers, and to keep this new cryptid alive. Of course a lot of people did believe that this video was legitimate, but this clearer look at these creatures proved to be divisive in the supernatural community.

Since their second appearance on camera, the Nightcrawlers have popped up sporadically in cryptid encounters, though usually with no video or photographic evidence. Notably, a couple in Carmel, Ohio reported seeing a creature that they described as being very similar to the Fresno Nightcrawlers. Similar, but with one big difference: the creature they saw was at least seven feet tall. A good deal taller than the small Nightcrawlers. Is it possible the Nightcrawlers are the young version of the Carmel Area Creature?

And what are the Fresno Nightcrawlers (and possibly the Carmel Area Creature) anyway? Of course there are the usual theories that these creatures are extraterrestrial in origin. There is also the theory that they come from another dimension. The belief is that they were either beamed down from a flying saucer or wandered through a wormhole through reality right into Jose's garden.

Many sceptics have tried to prove the Nightcrawlers are simply a hoax. We've spoken about the belief that they are digitally animated or puppets, but some non-believers have gotten more creative. Some say that they are a species of large bird, and the camera just couldn't catch their heads or necks and that their wings are tucked back.

Another real life animal theory is that they are deer walking on their hind legs. Personally, I think the idea of bipedal deer stalking suburban gardens in the dead of night is far more terrifying than the concept of extraterrestrial trousers.

The Fresno Nightcrawlers might be just a hoax that got out of hand. They might be from another planet or dimension. They might be an animal native to Earth that just hasn't been discovered by science yet. They might even be an advanced species of deer that has evolved to walk upright. Whatever they are, they are the newest cryptid on the scene.

Despite having only materialised into existence in 2007, having appeared in only two videos, and having only a handful of reported eyewitness accounts, they have captured the imagination of the monster-loving public. A quick Google search will bring up pages and pages of articles, videos, and podcasts discussing Fresno's most mysterious trousers, and even more pages of fan art and merchandise. Very impressive for a cryptid that lacks the years of reports, numerous sightings, and blurry photos of Bigfoot or Nessie! Surely it is only a matter of time before they have their big break in the mainstream, influencing some sort of movie or videogame like just the Flatwoods Monster or the Hopkinsville Goblins.

Perhaps what endeared the Fresno Nightcrawlers to the public was the fact that they appeared in a very normal neighbourhood and in a very normal garden. It made people think that strange beasts could appear in their own towns too. Also, how they look: like walking trousers. It's a simple design, but very memorable. These two things combined, trousers with a mind of their own taking a nighttime stroll through a normal guy's garden, it was just *Too Weird To Be Fake.*

The most mysterious thing about the Fresno Nightcrawlers though is their name: Nightcrawlers. They didn't crawl, they walked. The creatures were mostly leg, walking was pretty much all they *could* do. But I suppose the Fresno Night*walkers* just doesn't have the same ring to it.

MOTHMAN & FRIENDS

I've referenced him, and the events surrounding him, multiple times in this book already.

You've heard so many bits and pieces that you might be hitting the cover, rustling the pages (unless you're reading this on an e-reader, please don't damage your expensive technology), and shouting, "Just tell me about Mothman already!"

Well, they say to save the best for last. I can think of no better way to close out *Too Weird To Be Fake!* than recounting the bizarre events in Point Pleasant, West Virginia from 1966 to 1967. UFOs lit the sky, poltergeists terrorised locals, Men in Black stalked the streets, and at the centre of it all: **Mothman**. One of the strangest creatures ever described. King of the cryptids. Humanoid, bipedal, pitch black, winged, huge glowing red eyes. But what was the Mothman? Why was he here? And why did so much other weird stuff surround him?

On November 2, 1966, not too far from where Woodrow Derenberger first met Indrid Cold just over a week prior, five men were hard at work in a cemetery. The men were busy digging a grave for a funeral the next day. One man stopped digging to catch his breath and spotted something strange. He saw something moving in the nearby treeline. He alerted his fellow diggers, and they also saw movement. What was moving inside the cover of trees was too big to be an animal. It was almost too big to be *human*. What was even stranger was that it wasn't moving at ground level, it seemed to be flying at tree level. As the men tried to make sense of what they could be seeing, the creature suddenly flew from the treetops and right over their heads. Though the creature was moving at lightning fast speed, the men managed to catch a quick glimpse of it. They described it as a human-looking figure with a large pair of wings. This was the first sighting of Mothman.

Three days later, in the nearby town of Point Pleasant, Mothman would appear again. In Point Pleasant there was a place known as "the TNT Area". This was an area on the edge of town that was, during World War II, used for ammunition manufacturing. Along with the usual warehouse-type buildings, there were also many bunkers and igloo-like domed structures that were used for storage. In 1966, this small industrial area had been long abandoned and was mainly frequented by local teenage couples who were interested in military history (that's why they'd be out there, right?).

On November 15, not one but *two* teenage couples were in the TNT Area at midnight (it might have been tough to see the historic bunkers at that hour). Roger Scarberry was driving his squeeze Linda, his buddy Steve, and Steve's squeeze Mary, around the abandoned buildings and munitions domes. As they were driving, Linda suddenly let out a scream. "There's something out there!" she shrieked. Roger slammed on the breaks and calmed her down. She told him and her fellow passengers that she had seen a pair of big glowing red eyes looking at her out of the darkness. They thought her mind must have been just playing tricks on her, but then they saw it. In the darkness they saw what looked like a tall, slender, muscular man, at least seven feet in height. On his back, though, were a pair of folded wings. And of course, they all saw the huge red eyes.

It was standing near a fence, and had possibly gotten a wing caught on it. Roger thought about speeding off, but he couldn't. Whether he was simply too shocked to put pedal to the metal or whether the red eyes had some sort of hypnotic power is unknown. Steve managed to shout out to Roger, telling him to drive and breaking him out of his stupor. Roger didn't need to be told twice. He stepped on the ignition and got himself and his friends away from the winged figure as quickly as possible. As they fled, Mothman shambled towards the open door of an abandoned building, and the friends thought themselves safe.

But it wasn't over. After the car had driven on a bit, seemingly to safety, they saw the same creature by the side of the road again. Roger didn't stop to take a second look into those red eyes, he kept on driving. In the rearview mirror Roger saw the figure spread its wings and fly into the sky. After disappearing into the night, it reappeared chasing the car. Roger pushed the car to its limits, but Mothman easily kept up. As it flew behind the vehicle at speeds upwards of 100 miles an hour, the group inside the car heard a sound that was similar to a record being played too fast.

The friends feared what would happen if and when the winged beast managed to catch up to them. As they reached the populated area of Point Pleasant, though, Mothman landed in a field beside the road and took off running. According to the group, Mothman was much less graceful on foot than he was in the air, possibly explaining how he managed to get a wing snagged on a fence earlier.

Roger, Linda, Steve, and Mary were relieved that the chase was over but unsure of what to do now. Could they tell anyone? Would anyone believe them? They decided that they had to report it. They drove to the Point Pleasant Police Station and spoke to Deputy Sheriff Halstead. They expected to be laughed out of the building, but Halstead listened to them. The deputy sheriff knew these kids and didn't take them for troublemakers. After hearing their story, Halstead believed that something weird had definitely happened to these four out in the TNT Area. They were obviously scared when they arrived at the station and the story sounded too outlandish for them to have just made it up.

Halstead jumped in his cruiser and drove out to the TNT Area to see if he could find what the kids saw. Whether he truly believed that he was looking for a winged humanoid, or if he just expected to find some pranksters with a kite is unknown. Either way, he wanted to get to the bottom of this. He inspected what he could of the large area, but found nothing. Oddly though, his police radio experienced a strange malfunction while out there. Under different circumstances, it might not have been worth mentioning. But Halstead described the distortion on his radio as sounding like a record being played too fast.

The next day, November 16, a press conference was held and local reporters were told about the experience of the two couples in the TNT Area the night before. *The Point Pleasant Register* would print the story under the incredible headline of "Couples See Man-Sized Bird…Creature…Something!" Soon, the story spread from town to town and state to state, and the "Bird, Creature, Something" would be given a more catchy name. The creature was named after a villain from the classic 1960s *Batman* TV series starring Adam West. The creature was dubbed Mothman.

We talk about synchronicities a lot in the paranormal field, so I feel it worth mentioning that John Keel, who is best known for writing about Mothman and the events surrounding him, wrote an erotic Batman-inspired spoof novel that was released in 1966 titled *The Fickle Finger of Fate*. Could it be mere coincidence that the man who became best known for his Mothman work had just that very year released a book inspired by the protagonist of the series that the creature was named after? Truly the universe must have had Batman-related plans for this man, though it was more monster-based and less top-shelf X-rated pulp fan-fiction.

With Mothman now in the public mind, sightings continued. On the 16th of November, the same day as the press conference and the *Register* article, Marcella Benette and her husband were visiting friends near the TNT Area with their new baby. As they left their car and made their way towards their friend's house, they saw something appear behind the vehicle. It was as if it had been lying down on the road behind the car as it parked, and now rose up.

Marcella described what she saw as being taller than a man. It was a dark grey, and it seemed to have no head but had two large red eyes shining from near the top of its chest. Marcella gazed into these eyes and was frozen. Again, whether it was shock or some sort of hypnotic power is unknown. Marcella's husband, Raymond, believed that she was put into some sort of trance by the creature. A trance so intense that she dropped her baby that she was carrying. Luckily, the ground was soft and the child was unharmed by this unexpected drop. (Years later, the kid would have the privilege of replying to the tired "Were you dropped on your head as a baby?" with "Yes, but only because my mum was hypnotised by Mothman.")

Raymond rushed forward and scooped up his child, then managed to shake Marcella out of her trance. They ran to their friend's house and were let inside just as a pair of massive wings emerged from the back of the creature. Once safely indoors, they could hear the creature walking across the porch and saw red eyes looking through the windows. Mothman fled the scene before the police arrived.

That same night, a group of locals armed with guns and large butterfly nets stormed the TNT Area, looking for the creature. They searched the abandoned buildings, the domes, and the wild areas around the whole location, but found no Mothman. Some thought he must be hiding out somewhere else, others thought he must be living in the underground tunnels in the area, though many of these were boarded up and flooded. As they searched, a strange red light hung in the sky. From a UFO, or the gaze of the Mothman himself?

Marcella was traumatised by the incident (hardly surprising as it made her drop her child) and believed that Mothman would visit her home in the weeks after. She would describe feeling the same intense fear that she experienced the first time she saw the creature behind her car, almost as if Mothman radiated bad vibes. She would also say she could hear it outside her home at night. She described Mothman as producing a high-pitched sound that went right through her bones.

The next week, on November 24, multiple witnesses saw Mothman flying through the skies over the TNT Area. The very next day, Thomas Ury was driving not far from the TNT Area when he saw a tall humanoid with wings standing in a field. Thomas slowed down to get a better look at the odd figure, and as he did it spread its wings and raised into the air. What made this even stranger was that it never flapped its wings, it just levitated upwards. Thomas described it as taking off like a helicopter. Much like the incident with the two couples, Mothman started to chase Thomas' car.

Thomas decided to gun it to the police station, hoping to speed ahead of Mothman. Mothman didn't seem to want to catch Thomas, though. Thomas drove at seventy-five miles an hour, and Mothman would easily keep up and even fly over the top of his car and circle back to start the chase all over again, all the while never actually flapping its ten-foot-wide wings. It was almost like

Mothman was playing a game with poor Thomas. Mothman broke off the chase once again before he reached the general population. Thomas was so scared by this encounter that he couldn't go to his job that day. I'm sure that was an interesting call to his boss.

On November 27, eighteen-year-old Connie Carpenter was driving home from church at around 10.30 in the morning when she saw a man standing on a golf course. This man was very tall and dressed all in grey, and Connie thought it was quite strange that he was just standing there and not holding a golf club. That was until a pair of wings unfolded from his back and Connie realised that she wasn't looking at a man at all, but a Mothman.

It took off and flew straight for her car, barreling towards Connie's windscreen in a terrifying game of chicken. Mothman changed direction before collision, but before it did Connie got a good look at its face. She described it as indescribable. She mentioned its huge red eyes, that it was horrible looking, and that it resembled "something out of a science-fiction movie". Connie, perhaps because of her particularly close encounter with Mothman, suffered some type of eye infection for two weeks afterwards.

The world of the weirder than weird wasn't quite done with Connie just yet, though. Some weeks after her Mothman encounter, she was walking down a street in Point Pleasant when a black car pulled up beside her. A thin man in a black suit got out and told her to get in the car. Connie refused. The man tried to grab her, and a struggle ensued. Luckily, Connie managed to break free of his clammy grasp and ran home. Later, a note was slipped under her door that read, "Be careful, girl. I can get you yet." The Men in Black had arrived in Point Pleasant.

Soon after, in January 1967, Mary Hyre received her own visit from an MIB. Hyre was a journalist in town who ended up covering all the strange reports that locals were making. Maybe it was this area of reporting that made her a prime target for the black-suited baddies.

While at work one day, a memorable five-foot-tall man with an unfashionable bowl cut, thick glasses, and a black suit entered her office. If this short man had some sort of message for Mary, he quickly forgot it when he spotted her pen. The man was fascinated by the ballpoint pen on her desk, and he examined it as if he'd never seen one before. Mary, unnerved by this and the man's oddly hypnotising eyes, told him he could keep it. The man, overjoyed, let out a shrill and terrifying laugh then left her office with the pen in hand.

Several weeks later, Mary saw the short man again on a street outside of her work. When the man noticed her, he seemed alarmed. All of a sudden a black car sped around the corner, stopped, the little man jumped in, and the car drove off, thankfully without trying to abduct Mary. Even for a Man in Black encounter, this was a strange one. The MIB weren't done with Mary, though, and soon after she'd have another experience that was closer to what we've come to expect from the suited menace of UFO investigators everywhere.

Later in 1967, two identical men in black suits turned up at Mary's office. One of the twins told Mary, without emotion in his voice, that there had been a lot of UFO reports in Point Pleasant. He didn't need to tell Mary this; she was the one reporting it all. The same man asked what she would do if someone told her to stop reporting on the strange stories in town. Mary didn't even look up from her work, and responded like Arnold Schwarzeneggar in an 80s action movie. She told the Man in Black, "I'd tell them to go to Hell." There was no reply. Mary looked up from her work and both of the men had vanished.

Later that night, one of these men (or a very similar looking MIB) would turn up at the homes of UFO and Mothman witnesses claiming to be a reporter.

He made all he visited very uncomfortable with his unusual mannerisms and strange lines of questioning. His goal was unclear.

More MIB (and even a WIB (Woman in Black)) would soon flood into the town like a plague of the peculiar. Three men in black suits were reported visiting numerous houses late at night and asking odd questions in voices that lacked an accent under the guise of selling magazine subscriptions. They made no sales.

A woman dressed all in black visited many homes around the same time, claiming to be conducting a survey. She asked bizarre questions relating to family sizes and children. She even asked a woman in her 80s if she had any kids that were under six, as if she didn't have a grasp on human biology. She left in a car that had its licence plate obscured. A car driven by a man in a black suit.

It seemed like if you had seen Mothman or a UFO, were interested in them, or were even just unfortunate enough to live in Point Pleasant between 1966 and 1967, you would receive a visit from the MIB. But that wasn't all. Many local people who had seen the winged thing or a strange craft also ended up with haunted houses. After a sighting, witnesses would report unknown smells in their homes. They would see phantom lights floating around their rooms. Objects would go missing. Doors would unlock themselves. As if these people didn't have enough to worry about!

Strange activity wasn't just boxed into the small town, though. The weird has no interest in borders and boundaries, and it wasn't long before it started to spill out. In Spring of that year, a young man and woman were parked on an old disused road near Point Pleasant at around 10.00 PM.

They were both in the backseat, and while it's unclear exactly what they were doing, they were both butt naked. Things were going swimmingly until the sound of the squeaky backseat was broken by a low humming or buzzing. At first the man felt emasculated, believing the woman had brought some sort of electronic aid to the party. He soon realised that this wasn't the case. The woman was just as confused by the sound. And it seemed to be coming from outside of the car, not inside.

They wiped some condensation off one of the car windows and peered out into the dark night. As they looked out, they were nearly blinded by a sudden and intense blue light that shone in. The woman screamed, and they quickly scrambled back into their clothes. They thought, or perhaps hoped, that it was just the local police coming to move them on. As soon as they were clothed though, the light disappeared. The man and woman looked back outside, but could see no trace of what caused the light. They decided to head back to town. When they arrived, they realised that they had somehow lost two hours of time.

They thought about reporting the strange incident to the police, but decided that might not be the best idea. If they reported it, they'd have to explain what they were doing on that old road. And while that explanation might have put them in an embarrassing situation, what made things worse was that the woman in question had a husband. A husband that was not the man she was in the car with. They decided, to avoid an awkward situation and probable ass-kicking for the man, that they'd just try and forget about the whole thing.

Forgetting was hard, though. The next morning, they both awoke sunburnt over their entire bodies. The man got it even worse; his eyes had some sort of infection that caused them to swell shut, rendering him partially blind for two whole weeks.

What did they see on the old dirt road that night? The effect of the blue light had a similar effect on the man and woman as it did to Connie Carpenter when she had her very close encounter with Mothman. Was Mothman being a bit of a voyeur, and peeking in on this couple in their car? Mothman's gaze is always described as red, but could he have the ability to change eye colour? Or could he have a selection of coloured contacts? Maybe he wanted to be in disguise while he was being a Peeping Tom.

Over the coming months, while all manner of weird events were occurring almost in unison, Mothman sightings continued in and around Point Pleasant. Whether he was seen just chilling out in fields and on roofs, flying over buildings and chasing cars, or gliding through the TNT Area, the reports kept coming. Along with Mothman came UFO, MIB, and poltergeist reports, even a Bigfoot was possibly on the loose! Large animal tracks were discovered near the TNT area that looked suspiciously similar to the tracks found after Bigfoot sightings. It is feasible that these were Mothman tracks, and he just had really big feet. No one ever described his lower-half, as they were too distracted by the eyes and wings. Either way, all this strangeness brought the now legendary ufologist John Keel and former IFSB member Gray Barker to town.

Keel and Barker quickly got to work tracking down witnesses and collecting stories related to Mothman, strange lights in the skies, weird guys in suits stalking the streets, and once normal homes that now had problems with objects moving on their own accord. Both men would write about their findings and experiences in individual books. Keel would release his book *The Mothman Prophecies* in 1975, and it would later be adapted into a pretty okay, if inaccurate, film of the same name in 2002 starring Richard Gere.

Barker would release his book titled *The Silver Bridge* in 1970, and though it predated Keel's book by five years, it went largely unknown, though is now recognised as an underrated classic. Barker would later claim, perhaps with slight jealousy, that Keel was only in Point Pleasant because he told him about it. This is the ufologist equivalent of saying "I liked that band *before* they were famous."

December of 1967 would see the departure of Mothman, but before the year ended Keel claimed that over one hundred people in Point Pleasant had seen the red-eyed terror, and over *one thousand* had seen UFOs. Keel himself would see multiple UFOs during his time in town, and even saw a red and green craft landing in a ravine.

Mothman's exit was to be a dramatic one, as it coincided with a real life tragedy. On December 15, the Silver Bridge, which connected Point Pleasant to Gallipolis, collapsed into the Ohio River during rush hour. Forty-six people lost their lives in this tragic accident, and the community of Point Pleasant was shaken to its core.

Some people claimed that Mothman was in Point Pleasant *because* of this bridge collapse. Some believed he was a sort of omen or warning of imminent disaster. Others believed that he was a malevolent entity drawn here to enjoy the torment of humans. Some even believe that Mothman had some sort of physical hand in the bridge's collapse. Others believe that connecting a cryptid to a very real tragedy is in quite poor taste.

The actual cause of the collapse was found to be a faulty eyebar beam, and nothing to do with an anthropomorphic moth attacking the bridge with power tools in an act of sabotage. The fact that the bridge collapsed almost one year after the first Mothman sighting, and that there were no sightings afterwards, is certainly an interesting coincidence if nothing else.

There were unsubstantiated reports of Mothman sightings after the Silver Bridge collapse. There are even reported Mothman sightings around the world to this day. To paranormal fans, cryptozoologists, and ufologists, though, there is only one Mothman, and he belongs to Point Pleasant from 1966 to 1967.

With Mothman now departed, the town began to slowly return to normal. But the story didn't quite end there. With Barker and Keel's books released, the tale continued to grow. Keel's *Mothman Prophecies* in particular added a whole new element to the tale. An element that involved visions, predictions, and, of course, prophecies.

Now, you might be thinking to yourself, "I've heard a lot about *The Mothman Prophecies*, but what *were* these titular prophecies? Were there any, or was it just a catchy title?" While Mothman didn't write down any specific prophecies like a winged Nostrodamus, there is a reason why the book is called this.

Some might say that the appearance of Mothman itself was a prophecy that foreshadowed the imminent disaster of the bridge collapse. While that may be true, there are more elements to the story that could be considered prophetic, and they all relate to the Silver Bridge.

Before the disaster, a Mrs Thomas told John Keel and Mary Hyre about a recurring nightmare that she had. A nightmare that only began to haunt her dreams after she had seen a large humanoid figure gliding through the TNT area. In her nightmare, she saw people around the Ohio River, and crossing the Silver Bridge in such large numbers that the locals had to flee their homes. Though she couldn't work out what it meant, the appearance of strange figures invading her home and the inclusion of the Bridge would soon become apparent.

Mrs Thomas' dream seemed to be the start of a strange wave of nightmares in the town. Mary Hyre herself had a rather disturbing one that she shared with Keel. In it, she saw Christmas presents being washed away down an icy river. Given the date of the bridge collapse, December 15, it's not hard to imagine that some cars contained holiday gifts.

Around this time in early December, Keel would report that Point Pleasant had taken on a very weird vibe. People he'd come to have known during his time there would tell him that something didn't feel quite right anymore. It seemed like the town somehow knew that disaster was about to strike. It was Keel himself that would receive the most direct message concerning the imminent tragedy in Point Pleasant.

In the months and weeks prior to the disaster, strange things had begun happening to Keel and his work. He would receive phone calls that had no voice, just odd sounds like electronic beeps on the other end. Letters he was sending were being tampered with. Someone was impersonating him and even faked his death, claiming he died in a mine cave-in. When Keel would speak to newspapers and reporters, the footage would mysteriously become unusable and the audio tapes would be "accidently" deleted. It seemed that the Men in Black were up to their old tricks again.

As things began to intensify with the MIB, a strange entity known as Mr Apol gave Keel a message of disaster. It took some time to work out exactly what this message meant, but it seemed to be a warning that something terrible would happen on December 15. The warning seemed to be about a huge electrical blackout that would span the entire United States. The warning also suggested something more local. Keel began to fear that a factory along the Ohio River, close to Point Pleasant, would blow up. It was suggested that all of this would be synched up to the president lighting up the Christmas tree on the White House lawn.

Keel watched this festive ceremony on television, though he was not in the Christmas spirit. Keel was worried that the USA was on the brink of being plunged into a pitch-black *Mad Max* style apocalypse. As the president threw the switch, the tree lit up and...it stayed lit up. There was no blackout. The country was safe. Keel removed himself from the edge of his seat, and sat back, breathing a sigh of relief. It was all just some alien prank. Then an announcement came over the broadcast: a bridge had collapsed into the Ohio River during rush hour, more details to come.

There was a disaster on the date and the time that Keel had been warned about. It was even in the same area, but it hadn't been *the* disaster; there was no power cut and no explosion. How could this have happened? Had Keel misheard the messages he had been given? Had something been lost in translation? Was this a simple miscommunication between Keel and whatever had tried to warn him? Or had this been intentional? Had someone or something lied to him, prophesying the date and time of a disaster, but not giving Keel the correct details of what would happen, rendering him powerless to stop it? Who exactly had given him this prophecy anyway? Who, or what, was Mr Apol? Was he one of the Men in Black? One of Indrid Cold's fellow Lanulosians? A friend of Mothman? A prankster with a lucky guess?

Apol, who Keel received this prophecy of disaster from, was (what else) an interdimensional being. Though Keel would never actually meet Apol in the flesh, he would receive messages from him in letters, over the phone, and through alien abductees. Keel would even send Apol questionnaires to fill out in order to learn more about him. Apol's messages to Keel would contain predictions about all manner of things, like aeroplane crashes and popes, and some of them would come true.

Apol's prophecies of blackouts and explosions were given to Keel, but were not correct. Was this intentional? Was he having a bit of a joke at his expense? Was he also the person who had stolen Keel's identity, and even convinced several people he had died down a mine? Or, due to how he existed in our world, was he just unable to give an entirely accurate description of the events he saw unfold?

Keel believed that Apol and others of his kind were trapped in our time, and unable to tell the difference between past and future. He was, after all, correct about the date and the fact that something would happen on the Ohio River. Did Apol know something would happen, and he was just unable to understand what? And the question must be begged — was he connected at all to Indrid Cold, Mothman, the Men in Black, or any of the other weirdness that had besieged Point Pleasant?

Whatever Mr Apol was, if Keel is to be believed, he was capable of predicting the future with some degree of accuracy. If Keel's theory of Apol being confused about the flow of time in our world is correct, could this explain the errors he made in his December 15 predictions? Whatever the case may be, Mothman may have been the star of the show, but it was Mr Apol who truly put the *Prophecies* in *The Mothman Prophecies*.

The arrival of Mothman in Point Pleasant seemed to be the start of a thirteen-month saga of high strangeness that began on November 12, 1966 and ended with the collapse of the Silver Bridge on December 15, 1967. In this time, Point Pleasant got so weird that it made *Twin Peaks* look like just a nice normal town by comparison. But why did this happen? Why did such a gamut of paranormal and supernatural seem to come in the wake of this winged creature? And why did it arrive in Point Pleasant in the first place? Why did it leave after the bridge disaster? And what *even was* the Mothman?

Some sceptics have suggested that Mothman was simply a case of misidentification. They say that witnesses of Mothman saw a bird, specifically a sandhill crane (makes a change from the owl that usually gets blamed). There is certainly a population of sandhill cranes in Point Pleasant, and they are a very tall species of bird. If hit with a bright light, their eyes could definitely reflect a glow as a result. This theory falls apart when we consider the height of Mothman and the speed at which he could fly, neither of which match the sandhill crane. There is also the muscular body of Mothman, which is described as human (or close to it) and the sandhill crane is not only not ripped and buff, but also doesn't have a remotely human looking torso.

It seems unlikely that so many residents of the same town would mistake a bird for a bizarre-looking creature from outside of time and space. And while seeing a particularly large species of bird unexpectedly may be startling, I don't believe it would cause enough terror to make a mother drop her newborn baby.

That is unless this wasn't a *normal* sandhill crane at all. What if it was a mutant? The TNT Area was known to be quite dangerous and possibly bad for the environment. Many chemicals used in ammunition manufacturing back in WWII were extremely harmful and toxic; chemicals that may have leaked into the surrounding area and affected local wildlife. Could a regular, scrawny sandhill crane have found and taken a dip in a puddle of radioactive green goo and emerged a mutated and muscular version of itself, just like the *The Toxic Avenger*?

It could also explain the strange eye problems and skin burns many people experienced after seeing "Mothman"; the mutant sandhill crane could have been radiating dangerous energy as a side effect of its transmogrification. As amazing as this theory would be if it were true, even in a story about a Mothman, the Men in Black, and UFOs, a mutant crane seems pretty far-fetched.

Assuming hundreds of people didn't mistake a bird for a huge winged inhumanoid, what could Mothman have been?

Could he be an alien? With over a thousand people seeing UFOs in Point Pleasant during the thirteen-month spree of high strangeness, it's not a huge leap to imagine that Mothman was beamed down from one of these craft, then sucked back up after the bridge collapse. As we know by now, extraterrestrials have many forms. Some look almost human, some look like mechanical beings with elephant skin, and some even look like giant vegetables. When we consider this, an alien looking like a cross between a man and a moth doesn't sound too crazy. But why would a flying alien be sent down to Point Pleasant?

Could he be from another dimension? The town was practically besieged by all manner of weirdness. Could this be because Point Pleasant is in a location where the veil between this world and another dimension is thin? Could the veil, for some reason, have ripped open just enough to let Mothman, UFOs, poltergeists, the Men in Black, and more pour through? If so, then why did they all just politely return after the collapse of the Silver Bridge?

Could Mothman and pals have been from another dimension, and could they have been drawn here by the disaster of the Silver Bridge? This may sound odd given that they appeared more than a year *before* the event, but what if time works differently for creatures in different dimensions?

Evidence for this time theory may have occurred near Point Pleasant around the same time as Mothman first appeared. A woman was finishing up work in Gallipolis, just across the river from Point Pleasant, in November of 1966. She was outside of the office building where she was employed in the early evening, getting ready to go home. Suddenly, there was a bright flash in the sky, and a cylindrical craft descended silently and landed in the car park, not far from the woman.

After it was safely parked, what looked like two tall men with high cheekbones wearing coveralls walked out of it. They approached the woman, and in high-pitched voices they asked her name. They then asked where she was from, and where she worked. This was strange, but at least the woman could understand their questions. That was about to change. They then asked "What is your time?" The woman didn't know what they meant, but she knew they weren't asking for *the* time, which was around 8.00 PM. The question seemed to imply that time worked differently for these beings, and they needed to know more information about the time on Earth in order to adapt to it.

Some have even suggested that the reason why aliens, cryptids, and the MIB move in ways that appear very unusual is because they struggle to sync their bodies up with how time moves and works in our world. As strange as this may sound, it could offer an explanation for some of the weirder elements already discussed in this book. Elements such as the Hopkinsville Goblins falling in slow motion, the Veggieman's telepathic message that sounded sped up, and even the Sandown Clown's written message to the kids that was all out of order. If time works differently for these otherworldly beings, then could they have known about the disaster of the Silver Bridge and the devastation of the community *before* it even happened?

This time theory may explain why Apol was able to give his predictions to Keel. Even Woodrow Derenbeger thought that Indrid Cold was a time traveller of some sorts. We've already discussed the theory that the MIB are time travellers, but their connection to time goes further than that. They've been known to ask people unusual questions like "What is your time cycle?" again suggesting that they have a different perception of time than us humans. Could it be that all otherworldly creatures, monsters, beings and entities view and experience time differently from us humans?

If these creatures did know about the disaster in Point Pleasant in advance, then why were they attracted to it? Were they here to try and warn us? To try and stop it? Were they just here to enjoy the torment and sadness of us mortals?

201

Do these interdimensional creatures literally feed on some sort of psychic energy excreted by humans when we feel fear, sadness, and pain? Could this be why Apol gave Keel misleading information, so he could devour his feelings of anguish and failure?

The fact that Woodrow Derenberger met Indrid Cold just over a week before the first reported Mothman sighting in an area not far from Point Pleasant cannot be mere coincidence. Indrid arrived in a craft of some sort and claimed to be from a place called Lanulos that sounded to be in another galaxy. Whether this is a literal different planet located somewhere in the universe or whether it's a place in a different dimension is unknown.

When Indrid travelled here from wherever he came from, what if his craft ripped a new hole in space and time? What if all manner of strange creatures were able to pour through this hole before Indrid or one his colleagues were able to sew it shut? Were they able to round up these interdimensional invaders while the town was distracted by the tragedy of the unfortunate and unrelated bridge collapse?

Mothman and Point Pleasant have become legendary. Anyone who has an interest in the weird will eventually come across the story of this small town and what unfolded after the tall, dark, winged creature with red eyes that could not possibly exist took up residency in the TNT Area and began visiting locals. Despite the tragic end to the story, residents of Point Pleasant have embraced their town's amazing tale and capitalised on their legend. Every September, the town holds the Mothman Festival.

They have a parade, they have people in costume as the famous cryptid, they have people in black suits, they have speakers who have researched the story, and even people who were involved in the events when they happened.

They have bands, artists, food, stalls, vendors, and more. And while you're there, why not check out the Mothman Museum? You can see original reports and newspaper clippings from when the weirdness began. You can check out exhibits on John Keel, Mary Hyre, the MIB, and of course the star of the show himself, complete with a life-sized and witness-description-accurate Mothman replica. And, of course, you can't leave without getting your picture taken with the famous Mothman statue! A twelve-foot-tall shiny metallic recreation of the monster as he was described in the original reports, complete with large red eyes, washboard abs, and an ass that won't quit.

Whether Mothman was in Point Pleasant to terrorise them, to try and warn them of imminent disaster, or whether Mothman simply turned up randomly, will always be an interesting discussion to have. For the people of the town, though, Mothman has become a mascot, a symbol, and an attraction. They took a terrifying beast from another world and turned it into something they could celebrate. More people than ever catch the Mothman bug (no pun intended) and visit Point Pleasant simply because of what happened there between 1966 and 1967. The town has built a huge tourism industry around the weirdness that struck them and the monster that came to visit. Believers and sceptics alike go to Point Pleasant to this day to try and experience how it must have felt when the Men in Black stalked the streets, strange lights lit the sky, and Mothman made locals drop their babies.

All this would not be possible though without one basic fact. When people come to learn about Mothman, Point Pleasant, Indrid Cold, and all the other bizarre happenings here, they would not become fascinated by it to such a degree that they would travel from across the world to visit a festival that celebrates a monster without this one specific detail. When people hear about Mothman and the events surrounding him they are struck with one simple thought:

"This is *Too Weird To Be Fake!*"

EPILOGUE

So there it is, twenty true stories that are weirder than weird. Twenty stories that are simply too bizarre to have been made up.

Though these stories are unrelated, you may have noticed connections and common themes between many of them: noises like a record being played incorrectly, telepathic communication, electrical interferences, strange illnesses and injuries that seem similar to radiation poisoning, and of course the ever-present Men in Black. Can it be mere coincidence that so many stories, sometimes decades and continents apart, could share such similar elements? Or could it be that these stories are more connected than we think?

Could the creatures and beings in these stories not be coming from a variety of planets, dimensions, and realities…but the same place? Is there one location, wherever it may be, where silver goblins, massive amoebas, talking mongooses, extraterrestrial gnomes, and more reside? Are they travelling here physically in strange craft shaped like saucers, kerosene lamps, pyramids, cigars, and all varieties of shapes and sizes? Or are they arriving here from another dimension or reality through tears in the very fabric of space and time? In this case, are UFOs the vehicles they use to traverse these sci-fi wormholes?

Could they be even more connected than that? Could they be not only coming from the same place, but the same *thing*? Could these strange creatures not even be real in the traditional sense, but projections? Could a single being from another planet or dimension be projecting a variety of clowns, penguins, and blobs into our world? Are these projections purposely so unbelievable, unundertsandable, and ridiculous by design? What would be the purpose? Fun? Could Earth and all its inhabitants be the subject of an intergalactic, multidimensional, millenia-spanning prank? If we are, maybe it's best to just laugh along.

No matter what these creatures really are and where they're coming from, though, all the stories in this book have one big connection: the people in these stories did not expect to encounter something out-of-this-world. No one expected to see a tentacled humanoid by the Ohio River. No one expected to open their door to a three-legged monstrosity. No one expected to have their blood drained by a giant vegetable.

Most people in these stories had no interest in the unknown prior to experiences. Some had never even heard terms like UFO, alien, and cryptid before they met one. All the same, though, by accident or design, the unknown appeared to them. In telling their stories, many were subjected to ridicule. A recurring theme in several of the stories is the discussion of if they should even tell anyone what had happened to them. With this in mind, we have to wonder — how many people have had a strange experience and just never told anyone about it?

In John Keel's fantastic *Strange Creatures From Time and Space*, he states that someone within 200 miles of you has had an unexplainable experience. How many of your friends, family, coworkers, and neighbours have encountered the bizarre and just kept it to themselves?

A final element to consider in these stories is that they can seemingly happen to anyone. Whether you're a holidaying child on the Isle of Wight, a shepherdess in the hills of Bolivia, or a poultry farmer in Wisconsin, anyone and everyone can and does experience the extraordinary. And if it can happen to anyone, then it can happen to you.

Maybe you'll be out for a walk one day and suddenly end up having a conversation with a robotic two-headed pangolin without ever moving your lips. Maybe you'll be on the beach and see a crustacean-man scuttling back into his watery domain and be left with a nasty case of pinkeye for your trouble. Maybe you'll be driving home and in the middle of the road you'll see a creature you thought only existed in folklore being beamed up into a flying saucer from the golden age of sci-fi. Maybe after any one of these encounters you'll start noticing a trio of black suited men in the periphery of your vision and, knowing what you know now, hope that's where they'll stay.

No matter how it happens, if it does happen, what will you do? Will you share it with the world, knowing full well you may not be believed? Or will you keep it a secret until the end of your days?

What will you do when you have your own story that is...

Too Weird To Be Fake!

ACKNOWLEDGEMENTS & THANKS

This book would not exist without those who have tirelessly researched these subjects before me. The people who do what I only pretend to. The people who are there, on the scene, interviewing witnesses. The people who read hundreds of pages of dull documentation and try to make sense of it. The people who go through the evidence and put it all in context.

The real Mulders and the unsung heroes of the paranormal.

A bulk of this book was researched online and the following websites, blogs, journals, and podcasts were absolutely invaluable in its writing. Some provided small but important pieces of information, others became the main source for multiple chapters. A list of primary sources by chapter can be found at the end of the book, but all of these sites deserve special recognition:

All That's Interesting

American Hauntings

Anomalien

Astonishing Legends

BUFORA

Bridgeport Library

British Fairies

Burials and Beyond

Charleston Terrors

Conspiracy Corner

Cryptid Wiki

Cryptopia

Curious Archive

Dark Tales

Daily Yonder

Futility Closet

Gef: The Eighth Wonder of the

World

Hardcore Zen

Haunted Objects Podcast

Hellier

History

Infinity Explorers

It's Something

Last Podcast on the Left

Legends of America

Medium

Mysterious Britain

New World Explorers Society

ObscUrban Legend

Oregon Live

Paranormal Database

Portland Ghosts

Skeptoid

Spooky Isles

Strangeology

The Ghost In My Machine

The Pacific Sentinel

The Saucer Life

Visit Braxton

Washington Bigfoot

We Are the Mutants

Week In Weird

Thanks to Laura for believing in the book and listening to my constant ramblings about extra-, intra-, and ultra-terrestrials.

Thanks to Ella for meowing me out of the stupor induced by hours of research into the unknown.

Thanks to mum and dad for encouraging me to be the weirdo we all know today.

Thank you to all my friends for the crazy amount of support and encouragement I received throughout writing this book.

Thank you to Matt for the incredible cover art (admit it, it's why you picked this book up in the first place!).

Thank you to all the people who experienced something strange and decided to tell their story and not care about who believed them. I hope I did your stories justice.

Thanks to John Keel, Gray Barker, Albert Bender, Brad Steiger, and all the other big names in the world of ufology.

Special thanks to the Men in Black for not interfering with this book's writing (but please do pay me a visit, I'd love to meet you!).

And finally, thank *you.*

Thanks for taking a chance on a book that is admittedly quite out of the ordinary. I hope you enjoyed reading these stories as much as I enjoyed telling them. Whether you believed them all, thought they were nonsense, or something in between, I just hope you had fun. I know I did!

I'll see you all again in *2 Weird 2 Be Fake!*

ABOUT THE AUTHOR

-Photo by Fraser Kerr

"Please contact me if you're interested in joining the **Goths for the Appreciation of Bigfoot Society (GFTAOBS)**"

Martin R. Shaw is a writer and paranormal enthusiast from the North East of Scotland. He developed a fascination (some say obsession) with the supernatural at a young age after being exposed to cheesy paranormal recreation shows and X-Files marathons.

He writes about UFOs, cryptids and ghosts in a fun and engaging style, including plenty of jokes and pop culture references along the way.

MAIN SOURCES BY CHAPTER

The Indescribable Octoman & The Frog People:

https://obscurban-legend.fandom.com/wiki/Octoman

https://itsmth.fandom.com/wiki/Octoman

https://www.astonishinglegends.com/astonishing-legends/2020/10/30/the-octo-man-from-ohio

https://web.archive.org/web/20150509062027/http://www.americanmonsters.com/site/2015/02/indescribable-octo-man-kentucky-ohio-usa/

https://www.jahernandez.com/posts/green-clawed-beast-of-the-ohio-river

https://cryptidz.fandom.com/wiki/Loveland_Frogmen

https://charlestonterrors.com/the-loveland-frogman-ohios-most-famous-cryptid/

https://frogmanfestival.com/

The Inhumanoids - Barton M. Nunnelly: Page 40

Sam: The Sandown Clown:

https://bufora.org.uk/documents/BUFORAJournalVolume6No.5JanFeb1978.pdf

https://www.cryptopia.us/site/2018/11/sam-the-sandown-ghost-clown-england/

https://obscurban-legend.fandom.com/wiki/The_Sandown_Clown

https://www.spookyisles.com/the-sandown-clown-fact-or-fiction/

https://www.curiousarchive.com/sam-the-sandown-clown-alien-man-in-black-or-folie-a-deux/

https://theghostinmymachine.com/2022/05/30/encyclopaedia-of-the-impossible-sam-the-sandown-clown/

BUFORA Journal - January/February 1978

Mysteries Of The Unknown - The UFO Phenomenon: Page 71

The Last Podcast On The Left - Relaxed Fit: Single-Use Cryptids

Attack of the Hopkinsville Goblins:

https://www.history.com/news/little-green-men-origins-aliens-hopkinsville-kelly

https://cryptidz.fandom.com/wiki/Hopkinsville_Goblins

https://darktales.blog/2019/05/10/the-hopkinsville-goblins/

The Inhumanoids - Marton M. Nunnelly: Page 255

UFOs The Definitive Casebook - John Spencer: Page 36

Strangers From The Sky - Brad Steiger: Page 10

Mysteries Of The Unknown - The UFO Phenomenon: Page 64

Braxxie: The Flatwoods Monster:

https://www.history.com/news/flatwoods-monster-west-virginia

https://braxtonwv.org/the-flatwoods-monster/

https://cryptidz.fandom.com/wiki/Flatwoods_Monster

https://cryptozoologycryptids.fandom.com/wiki/Flatwoods_Monster

The Inhumanoids - Barton M. Nunnelly: Page 251

Strangers From The Skies - Brad Steiger: Page 8

They Knew Too Much About Flying Saucers - Gray Barker: Page 11

The Not-So-Little Green Man:

https://obscurban-legend.fandom.com/wiki/Badajoz_UFO_Creature

https://cryptidz.fandom.com/wiki/Badajoz_UFO_Creature

https://www.infinityexplorers.com/badajoz-ufo-incident-green-alien/

https://anomalien.com/the-badajoz-ufo-incident-mysterious-encounter-with-a-green-alien-in-spain/

https://profilbaru.com/article/UFO_sightings_in_Spain

Flying Saucer Review - Vol. 23

Albert Bender & The Men in Black; A Villainous Origin Story:

https://bportlibrary.org/hc/authors/bridgeports-ufo-legacy-men-in-black-and-the-albert-k-bender-story/

https://www.ctpost.com/opinion/article/MIB-Mad-in-Bridgeport-Men-in-Black-The-legacy-10419913.php

https://wearethemutants.com/2019/07/16/harbingers-of-paranoia-how-the-men-in-black-infiltrated-the-ufo-phenomenon/

https://www.history.com/news/men-in-black-real-origins

https://news.lib.wvu.edu/2021/05/25/gray-barker-and-the-men-in-black-they-knew-too-much-about-flying-saucers/

The Last Podcast On The Left - Episodes 323, 324, 325

The Saucer Life - Of all the Things to Wish upon a Person

They Knew Too Much About Flying Saucers - Gray Barker: Page 109

The Inhumanoids - Barton M. Nunnelly: Page 217

The Real Men in Black - Nick Redfern: Page 21, 197, 209, 221

UFOs The Definitive Casebook - John Spencer: Page 14

Mysteries Of The Unknown - The UFO Phenomenon: Page 77

The Swedish Jelly Blobs:

https://www.cryptopia.us/site/2018/05/terrible-flying-jelly-bags-sweden/

https://vocal.media/futurism/attack-of-the-jellied-whatsits

https://villains.fandom.com/wiki/Domsten_Blobs

https://aliens.fandom.com/wiki/Domsten_Blob

https://cryptidz.fandom.com/wiki/Domsten_Blobs

Strangers From The Skies - Brad Steiger: Page 45

UFOs The Definitive Casebook - John Spencer: Page 88

Strange Creatures from Time and Space - John Keel: Page 145

Abducted by Intergalactic Robots:

https://www.cryptopia.us/site/2010/02/pascagoula-alien-abductors-mississippi-usa/

https://www.washingtonpost.com/history/2019/06/26/i-floated-inside-man-returns-site-ufo-abduction-it-gets-historical-marker/

https://eu.clarionledger.com/story/news/2020/07/13/pascagoula-ufo-alien-abduction-case-interview-recording-has-surfaced/3264064001/

https://cryptidz.fandom.com/wiki/Pascagoula_Elephant_Men

UFO Contact At Pascagoula - Charles Hickson, Willian Mendez: Page 26

UFOs The Definitive Casebook - John Spencer: Page 59

The Mothman Prophecies - John Keel: Page 235

Gef: The Talking Mongoose:

http://gefmongoose.blogspot.com/p/the-story-of-gef.html

https://burialsandbeyond.com/2019/12/13/gef-the-ghostly-mongoose/

https://theghostinmymachine.com/2018/02/19/unresolved-gef-talking-mongoose-dalby-spook/

https://www.mysteriousbritain.co.uk/hauntings/gef-the-talking-mongoose/

https://medium.com/illumination/the-bizarre-case-of-gef-the-talking-mongoose-df4c69131755

https://creativity.fandom.com/wiki/Gef_the_Mongoose

https://www.mentalfloss.com/article/71816/strange-story-gef-talking-mongoose

https://www.spookyisles.com/who-was-gef-the-talking-mongoose/

The Last Podcast On The Left - Episode 409

The Vampiric Veggieman:

https://newworldexplorerssociety.blogspot.com/2022/04/the-vegetable-man.html

https://www.cryptopia.us/site/2016/07/vegetable-man-west-virginia-usa/

https://cryptidz.fandom.com/wiki/Veggieman

https://itsmth.fandom.com/wiki/Veggieman

https://www.futilitycloset.com/2011/03/06/the-devils-snare/

Gray Barker's Newsletter No. 5

Alien Visitors - Brad Steiger: Page 57

Rumble in Bolivia: The Shepherdess versus The Sheep Slayer:

https://www.cryptopia.us/site/2018/09/potosi-sheep-slayer-bolivia/

https://www.infinityexplorers.com/the-mysterious-encounter-with-a-violent-alien-who-slaughtered-a-flock-of-sheep/

https://cryptidz.fandom.com/wiki/Potosi_Sheepslayer

The Missouri Alien Penguins:

https://www.strangeology.com/post/alien-casefile-the-tuscumbia-space-penguins

https://www.cryptopia.us/site/2011/10/space-penguins-of-tuscumbia-missouri-usa/

https://cryptidz.fandom.com/wiki/Tuscumbia_Space_Penguins

https://obscurban-legend.fandom.com/wiki/Space_Penguins_of_Tuscumbia

https://anomalien.com/tuscumbia-aliens-claude-edwards-story/

https://knewcastle.wordpress.com/2020/07/20/myth-monday-1967-the-year-the-green-space-penguins-made-contact/

Indrid Cold: The Grinning Man:

https://dailyyonder.com/woodrow-derenberger-and-the-legend-of-indrid-cold/2021/12/03/

https://www.encyclopedia.com/science/encyclopedias-almanacs-transcripts-and-maps/derenberger-woodrow

https://cryptidz.fandom.com/wiki/Indrid_Cold

https://www.spookyisles.com/gurning-man-glasgow/

https://www.glasgowlive.co.uk/news/glasgow-news/glasgow-ghosts-meet-gurning-man-20266535

The Saucer Life - A Cold Day in West Virginia

The Inhumanoids - Barton M. Nunnelly: Page 183

Strange Creatures from Time and Space - John Keel: Page 182

The Mothman Prophecies - John Keel: Page 63, 79, 139, 156

The Three-legged Enfield Monster:

https://medium.com/@chrisdarkes/strangers-in-the-night-156983eb0d7d

https://cryptozoologycryptids.fandom.com/wiki/Enfield_Horror

https://villains.fandom.com/wiki/Enfield_Horror

https://www.cryptopia.us/site/2010/03/enfield-horror-illinois-usa/

https://www.newspapers.com/newspage/30409597/

http://www.cryptozoonews.com/ill-ass/

https://news.google.com/newspapers?nid=1955&dat=19730822&id=hgsrAAAAIBAJ
&sjid=cZoFAAAAIBAJ&pg=3792,885792

https://en.wikipedia.org/wiki/Enfield_Monster

Out Of This World Pancakes:

https://www.cultofweird.com/ufo-sightings/wisconsin-alien-pancakes/

https://journalnews.com.ph/bizarre-ufo-encounter-of-us-farmer-three-aliens-gave-him-pancakes/

http://hardcorezen.info/alien-pancakes/7894

https://medium.com/@brknylmn/pancakes-from-space-april-18-1961-c6c825bd6a8f

UFOs The Definitive Casebook - John Spencer: Page 42

Batsquatch: The Flying Bigfoot:

https://cryptidz.fandom.com/wiki/Batsquatch

https://www.oregonlive.com/entertainment/2021/08/half-bat-half-sasquatch-nw-legend-explored-in-batsquatch-of-mount-st-helens.html

https://pacsentinel.com/batsquatch/

https://portlandghosts.com/the-story-of-the-batsquatch-the-terror-that-mount-st-helens-awoke/

https://washingtonbigfoot.com/2019/04/04/legend-of-batsquatch/

https://www.strangeology.com/post/cryptid-casefile-the-ahool

https://cryptidz.fandom.com/wiki/Ahool

American Monsters - Linda S. Godfrey: Page 52

The Inhumanoids - Barton M. Nunnelly: Page 155

The Finnish Space Gnome:

https://journalnews.com.ph/remarkable-ufo-humanoid-incident-near-imjarvi-finland/

http://www.ufoevidence.org/Cases/CaseSubarticle.asp?ID=744

http://forteana.freeservers.com/page2.html

https://paranormal-strange.fandom.com/wiki/Imjarvi_Goblin

https://www.howandwhys.com/finnish-dyatlov-pass-ufo-case-of-lake-imjarvi/

https://ufoac.com/an-alien-in-finland.-dyatlov-pass-in-finnish.html#gsc.tab=0

https://caballodetroy.medium.com/the-finnish-case-b81618a81830

Flying Saucer Review - Vol. 16

Alien Visitors - Brad Steiger: Page 40

UFOs The Definitive Casebook - John Spencer: Page 96

The Creepiest Children: Black-eyed Kids:

https://columnsfairmontstate.com/2858/conspiracy-corner/conspiracy-corner-black-eyed-kids/

https://www.tbsnews.net/splash/legend-black-eyed-children-55705

https://web.archive.org/web/20151208221117/http://www.reporternews.com/news/columnists/brian-bethel/brian-bethel-recounts-his-possible-paranormal-encounter-with-beks-ep-384772497-348207271.html

https://weekinweird.com/2016/01/28/witness-report-i-let-the-black-eyed-children-into-my-home-and-now-im-slowly-dying/

The Last Podcast On The Left - Episode 451

Living Trousers: The Fresno Nightcrawlers:

https://paranorms.com/fresno-nightcrawler/

https://www.strangeology.com/post/cryptid-casefile-the-fresno-nightcrawlers

https://skeptoid.com/episodes/4826

https://thebusinessjournal.com/more-than-fresno-famous-how-the-nightcrawler-captured-the-worlds-imagination/

https://cryptidz.fandom.com/wiki/Fresno_Nightcrawler

https://www.theodysseyonline.com/fresno-nightcrawlers

Fact or Faked: Paranormal Files - Season 1 Episode 2

Mothman & Friends:

https://www.americanhauntingsink.com/moth

https://www.legendsofamerica.com/west-virginia-mothman/

https://allthatsinteresting.com/mothman

https://www.mothmanmuseum.com/

https://www.mothmanfestival.com/

The Mothman Prophecies - John Keel: Page 20, 73, 107, 123, 129, 170

Strange Creature from Time and Space - John Keel: Page 221

American Monsters - Linda S. Godfrey: Page 63

The Real Men in Black - Nick Redfern: Page 53

The Inhumanoids - Barton M. Nunnelly: Page 139

The Last Podcast On The Left - Episodes 323, 324, 325

The Haunted Objects Podcast - Defending The Mothman

The Saucer Life - Mothman Unplugged, The Silver Bridge, John Keel and The Mothman Prophecies, An Apol a Day

Printed in Dunstable, United Kingdom